INTERNATIONAL TRADE AND LENDING

Michael B. Connolly

215636

382.1

C 752

Library of Congress Cataloging in Publication Data

Connolly, Michael B. (Michael Bahaamonde), 1941–
    International trade and lending.

    Bibliography: p.
    Includes index.
    1. Commerce. 2. Loans, Foreign. I. Title.
HF1411.C5775 1985   382.1   84-26354
ISBN 0-03-071166-5 (alk. paper)

Published in 1985 by Praeger Publishers
CBS Educational and Professional Publishing, a Division of CBS Inc.
521 Fifth Avenue, New York, NY 10175 USA

© 1985 by Praeger Publishers

All rights reserved

56789 052 987654321

Printed in the United States of America on acid-free paper

INTERNATIONAL OFFICES

Orders from outside the United States should be sent to the appropriate address listed below. Orders from areas not listed below should be placed through CBS International Publishing, 383 Madison Ave., New York, NY 10175 USA

Australia, New Zealand
Holt Saunders. Pty. Ltd.. 9 Waltham St.. Artarmon. N.S.W. 2064, Sydney, Australia

Canada
Holt, Rinehart & Winston of Canada. 55 Horner Ave., Toronto, Ontario, Canada M8Z 4X6

Europe, the Middle East, & Africa
Holt Saunders. Ltd.. 1 St. Anne's Road. Eastbourne, East Sussex, England BN21 3UN

Japan
Holt Saunders. Ltd.. Ichibancho Central Building. 22-1 Ichibancho, 3rd Floor, Chiyodaku, Tokyo, Japan

Hong Kong, Southeast Asia
Holt Saunders Asia. Ltd.. 10 Fl. Intercontinental Plaza, 94 Granville Road, Tsim Sha Tsui East, Kowloon, Hong Kong

Manuscript submissions should be sent to the Editorial Director, Praeger Publishers, 521 Fifth Avenue, New York, NY 10175 USA

PREFACE

This short text explores international trade theory. It is based on a course I have given over a number of years. As in the classroom, I have tried to keep things simple yet complete. For this reason the book relies primarily upon simple geometric analysis. A short, self-contained legend accompanies each graph as an aid to the reader. In addition, the conclusion section in each chapter highlights the main points developed.

I learned international economics from Robert Mundell, Harry Johnson, and Lloyd Metzler at the University of Chicago. I would like to acknowledge my debt to these teachers as well as to Arnold Harberger and Larry Sjaastad from whom I have learned much. At Harvard, I learned further about the theory of international trade from Gottfried Haberler.

CONTENTS

LIST OF FIGURES

INTRODUCTION

This book attempts to provide a succinct treatment of the pure theory of international trade. At the same time, it incorporates into the body of trade theory problems involving borrowing and lending over time. Chapters 1 and 2 sketch the Ricardian theory of comparative advantage and apply it to customs union theory, problems of growth, differences in the relative sites of countries, and international transfers of income. Chapter 3 sets forth the essential elements of the Heckscher-Ohlin trade model. Its basic propositions—(1) the pattern of comparative advantage is determined by relative factor endowments and (2) trade equalizes factor prices—are treated in considerable detail. Chapter 4 derives the conditions of production and consumption optimality and points out problems that may arise in a trade context when decreasing opportunity costs are present. Chapters 5 and 6 derive offer curves from production frontiers and indifference maps and apply them to the theory of tariffs and quotas and to problems of trade equilibrium and stability. Chapters 7 and 8 outline the Fisherian approach to foreign lending as trade over time. The one-to-one correspondence between capital theory, involving exchange over time, and trade theory, involving exchange at the same point in time, is stressed throughout. The Fisherian apparatus is then applied to the analysis of taxes and quantitative controls on foreign lending.

With few exceptions the text relies primarily upon simple geometric analysis, resorting as little as possible to arithmetic arguments. Each graph is accompanied by a short legend that allows for skimming by advanced readers and serves as a summary for others. In addition, I have attempted to make the points verbally in a simple, coherent manner. I hope the enterprise was successful.

ONE

THE CLASSICAL TRADE MODEL

At the origin of the modern theory of international trade, two questions were left unanswered. First, apart from trade in natural resources, how is it that apparently underdeveloped countries can manage to successfully engage in trade with technically more advanced nations? Second, does trade lead to gains in welfare? David Ricardo (1772–1823) has come to enjoy the reputation of the pioneer who successfully led to the answers to these questions. In 1817 he demonstrated in his celebrated *Principles of Political Economy and Taxation* that it is relative, not absolute, efficiency that brings about trade and that countries tend to gain by specializing in the production of goods in which they have a comparative advantage by exporting them for goods in which they have a comparative disadvantage. As is true today, it was typical to raise both positive questions having to do with why things happen as they do as well as the normative question of why things should be as they are.

This chapter lays the foundations of the simple Ricardian theory of comparative advantage. Its purpose is twofold: to familiarize the reader with the economic reasoning behind such propositions and to bring the classical trade model to bear upon some important problems such as the gains from trade, economic growth, and the different sizes of nations in an international setting. Finally, the results of some empirical tests of the classical model will be presented and discussed.

THE RICARDIAN ECONOMY

For simplicity it is assumed that the world is composed of two countries, America and Europe. We will use the letters A and E to represent the home and foreign countries, respectively, thereby identifying with America as the home country. In addition, suppose that there are only two commodities, bread and wine, indicated by the letters X and Y, as well as only one single factor of production, labor (L). An American worker is assumed to be identical to a European worker except for nationality. The context in which the discussion begins involves, in short, two countries with their respective labor forces and the two commodities of bread and wine.

There is one element missing from the picture, namely, techniques of production. In particular, we must know how efficiently American workers can produce bread and wine during any given period of time. Let us measure the average productivity per week of American labor in producing wine as a_y and in producing bread as a_x and assume that these average productivities are constant. To take an example, for a week's worth of effort, each worker in America can produce either 50 loaves of bread or 25 bottles of wine. Furthermore, these average productivities are constant; so taking one extra American from the vineyards and putting that individual in the bakery will always cause the weekly output of wine to fall by 25 bottles and that of bread to rise by 50 loaves. If the labor force of A were composed of 100 individuals, the maximum output of bread would be 5,000 loaves, and the maximum production of wine would be 2,500 bottles. In the first instance all labor is employed in the bread industry; in the second all work in the wine industry. By shuffling labor from the bread to the wine industry, America can thus convert two loaves of bread into a bottle of wine. This ratio, 2:1, is the rate of technical transformation in production and must equal the relative price ratio in America in the absence of foreign trade.

If the market rate of exchange exceeded two loaves of bread per bottle of wine, a tendency to specialize in the production of wine would tend to occur, whereas if the market price fell short of two, specialization in bread would tend to emerge, thereby eliminating any possible divergence in the two rates. This is so since producers can realize profits in diverting resources whenever the market price diverges from the marginal technical rate of production. The tendency to specialization, however, drives the market price back to the rate determined by the production conditions.

In the simple Ricardian framework the equilibrium rate at which one commodity exchanges for another in the absence of trade is thus determined solely by the ratio of the average productivities of labor in the wine and bread industries: a_y/a_x, or $25/50 = \frac{1}{2}$ in the example taken above. By moving one laborer from the wine industry, a loss of a_y bottles of wine per week results, whereas the individual's employment in the bread industry gives rise to an extra weekly output of a_x loaves. Naturally, then, the opportunity cost of bread in terms of wine foregone is a_y/a_x—that is, an extra loaf of bread has an opportunity cost of one-half bottle of wine. This ratio, in turn, reflects the market price in America at autarky, or self-sufficiency. A bottle of wine costs two loaves of bread, or a loaf of bread costs one-half bottle of wine.

We can summarize the simple Ricardian system for the closed economy in algebraic form. The labor force in America represents the initial resource endowment of the country. In turn, it must be divided between the bread (X) and wine (Y) industries, or

$$L_x+L_y=L_0, \tag{1.1}$$

With unemployment $L_x+L_y\leq L_0$. We are ruling out until later the problem of unemployment.

The technical conditions are given by the average productivities of labor in the two industries, or

$$Y=a_yL_y \tag{1.2}$$

and

$$X=a_xL_x. \tag{1.3}$$

This means simply that the output in each industry equals the average productivity of a laborer times the number of laborers employed in the industry concerned. Substituting equation 1.1 into 1.2, and 1.3 into the resulting equation gives the *production possibility frontier* for America:

$$Y=a_yL_0-(a_y/a_x)X. \tag{1.4}$$

The production frontier (equation 1.4) summarizes the maximum amounts of Y that can be produced for any particular level of production of X, given the average productivities of labor and the level of the labor force. It thus brings together the technical conditions of production and basic resource constraint faced by the economy. Further, it gives us the rate at which bread is transformed into wine, or

$$\frac{dY}{dX}=-a_y/a_x. \tag{1.5}$$

While this rate is frequently called the *marginal rate of transformation in production,* it is constant in the Ricardian model because the average productivities do not vary. In short, we have constant opportunity costs in production, and the relative price of bread in terms of wine is a_y/a_x—for example, an extra loaf of bread costs one-half bottle of wine when $a_y/a_x=\frac{1}{2}$.

The production functions of the wine and bread industry are drawn in the upper left- and lower right-hand quadrants, respectively, of Figure 1-1. The functions are linear since the average productivities of labor (their slopes) are assumed to be constant. The resource constraint for the economy is indicated in the lower left-hand quadrant. Its end points represent the employment of all labor in one or the other industry and are, therefore, equidistant from the origin, 0. Further-more, the slope of the resource constraint equals -1 for the simple reason that if an extra laborer is to be employed in the wine industry, total employment re-maining the same, one less worker must be employed in the bread industry. By taking the various combinations of labor allocations indicated along the resource constraint, and reading off the corresponding amounts of bread and wine produced, the production frontier in the upper right-hand quadrant is derived. Its end points represent the maximum amounts of output in a particular indus-try if all labor were employed in that industry. Once again, its slope equals the ratio of the average productivities of labor—a_y/a_x—since this is the rate at which wine can be transformed into bread by shuffling resources about.

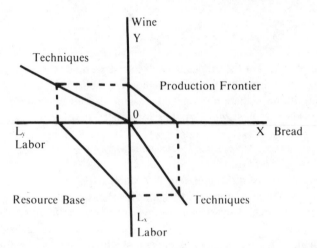

FIGURE 1-1. Ricardian System: Closed Economy. In the lower left-hand quadrant, the resource base of the Ricardian economy is indicated. The dis-tance along the two axes equals the labor endowment of the economy, and the slope of the line equals -1 since one more worker employed in the wine indus-try implies one less in the bread industry. The amounts of wine and bread capable of being produced are indicated in the upper left- and lower right-hand quad-rants. Since the average productivities of labor are assumed constant in both in-dustries, the production functions are straight lines. The production frontier in the upper right-hand quadrant is derived from the production functions and the resource base. Its slope is minus the ratio of the average productivities, a_y/a_x, since one worker diverted to the wine industry causes a loss of a_x loaves of bread and a gain of a_y bottles of wine. This rate gives the rate of transforma-tion in production in the economy and is constant since the average productivi-ties are constant. Furthermore, since relative prices must conform to this rate, and it is constant, prices are independent of demand conditions in equilibrium.

Since the ratio of the average productivities is also constant, the production frontier is a straight line. In the absence of trade the relative price ratio will also equal the slope of the production frontier; otherwise the market rates of exchange would differ from the rates of transformation in production, implying that profits could be made by moving toward the production of only one of the goods. This tendency toward complete specialization would, however, push market prices back into line with the opportunity costs of production. In short, provided that both goods are produced, the relative price ratio is determined in equilibrium solely by supply conditions. Demand is entirely irrelevant, as can be seen by choosing different demand patterns along the production frontier.

ABSOLUTE AND COMPARATIVE ADVANTAGE

The European economy can be summarized in the same manner. If we indicate the average productivities of European labor in the bread and wine industries by a_x^* and a_y^*, respectively, and the respective levels of production by X^* and Y^*, the production frontier of Europe is, similarly,

$$Y^* = a_y^* L_0^* - (a_y^*/a_x^*) X^*,$$

where L_0^*, is the size of the labor force in Europe.

The corresponding rate of transformation is

$$\frac{dY^*}{dX^*} = -a_y^*/a_x^*.$$

In the absence of trade the market price in Europe must also reflect the rate of transformation; so a_y^*/a_x^* indicates the price of bread in terms of wine.

Now, suppose European labor has a lower average productivity than American labor both in bread and wine production. That is, assume that $a_x^* < a_x$ in the bread industry and that $a_y^* < a_y$ in the wine industry; America enjoys an absolute advantage in the production of both goods. Is it possible for trade to exist between the two countries? Is Europe not too inefficient to compete in the markets of America? The answer is no because it is relative, and not absolute, advantage that establishes trade. By *relative* advantage, we mean the ratios of the average productivities in the two countries—or a_y^*/a_x^* and a_y/a_x. The relative or comparative advantages are determined by these ratios because they reflect the relative price of the two commodities in each country before trade. If, for instance $a_y^*/a_x^* > a_y/a_x$, European labor is relatively more efficient in the production of wine (Y), and this comparative efficiency is reflected in the cheaper price of wine in Europe. When the possibility of trade arises, Europe will consequently have a comparative advantage in wine, whereas America will have a comparative advantage in bread. Each will export the good in which it enjoys a comparative advantage and import the good in which it has a comparative disadvantage.

For example, consider the following average productivity of labor data:

	America	Europe
Wine	25	20
Bread	50	30

America has an absolute advantage in both wine production—since 25 > 20—and bread production—since 50 > 30—but Europe has a comparative advantage in wine production since 20/30 > 25/50. In the absence of trade a bottle of wine would cost only one and one-half loaves of bread in Europe, whereas a bottle of wine would cost two loaves in America. Consequently, Europe will export wine to America. On the other hand, a loaf of bread would cost one-half bottle of wine in America and two-thirds bottle in Europe before trade, so America exports bread to Europe.

The discussion of absolute and comparative advantage can be treated in the same graphical framework used for the closed economy (see Figure 1–2). As before, the sizes of the labor forces are indicated by the distance along either axis in the lower left-hand quadrant. As drawn, the labor force in Europe is larger than that of America. The production functions of the two countries are in the opposite upper left- and lower right-hand quadrants. Their slopes equal, once again, the average productivities of labor in bread and wine in the two countries. Notice two things, however: the average productivity of labor in A exceeds that in E in both industries; and second, the relative productivity of European labor in wine exceeds the relative productivity of American labor in wine. This is the geometric equivalent of the condition that America has an absolute advantage in the production of both goods—or $a_x > a_x^*$; $a_y > a_y^*$—but has a comparative advantage in the production of bread—$a_x/a_y > a_x^*/a_y^*$—or as stated in the text: $a_x/a_x^* > a_y/a_y^*$. In short, American labor is relatively less efficient in the production of wine.

The resulting production frontiers in the upper right-hand quadrant, AA' and EE', have different slopes, reflecting the difference in market prices in the absence of trade. In particular, the slope of AA' exceeds that of EE', implying that bread is relatively cheaper in A than in E. By the same token, wine is relatively cheaper in E than in A. Consequently, A has a comparative advantage in bread, E in wine; and both export the commodity in which their comparative advantage lies in exchange for imports of the other commodity.

TRADE EQUILIBRIUM

This does not tell us at what price the goods will exchange once trade occurs, nor does it tell us the exact number of loaves of bread that America exports and

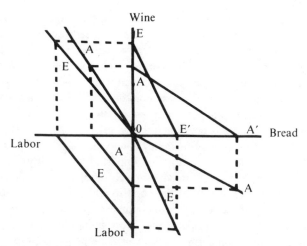

FIGURE 1–2. Pattern of Comparative Advantage. The pattern of comparative advantage is determined by the price ratios that would reign in the absence of trade. The labor forces and production functions of America and Europe are drawn as before. Notice that while the average productivity of labor in America exceeds that of European labor in both industries, it is relatively greater in the bread industry. As a consequence the autarkic price of bread is cheaper in America. Equivalently, wine is cheaper in Europe. In short, America has a comparative advantage in bread, whereas Europe has a comparative advantage in wine.

the number of bottles of wine it imports. We are not far, however, from the answers to these questions. The pretrade relative prices determine the pattern of comparative advantage, but they cannot alone give us the equilibrium price ratio once trade occurs. They are useful, however, because they serve as limits that cannot be exceeded by the terms of trade. For instance, if a bottle of wine costs two loaves of bread in America, and one loaf in Europe before trade, it would not be possible for a price of three loaves to emerge after trade. Why not? Because both *A* and *E* would wish to export wine, and since one's exports are the other's imports in a two-country world, this would be contradictory. Both simply cannot have a comparative advantage in the same good.

It follows that the pretrade price ratios serve as limits between which the trade price ratio must lie. Some intermediate price ratio might well do the trick. One might guess that we can call upon the familiar workhorse of economics, the law of supply and demand, to get our result. And indeed we can, for the *equilibrium price ratio* is reached when the number of bottles of wine the Europeans wish to export just equals the number of bottles Americans wish to import. Or equivalently, the equilibrium terms of trade are those that equate the American demand for imports of wine and the European supply of exports of wine. If, on the contrary, export supplies of American bread exceeded import demand in Europe, the relative price of bread would tend to fall, thereby eliminating the excess supply of bread on the world market. Note that owing to Mill's law of reciprocal demand, the situation just described would imply that export supplies of wine from Europe fall short of import demand in America, and the disequilibrium is reached by an increase in the relative price of wine. It is one and the same thing since there is only one relative price after trade. Thus the terms of trade must satisfy two conditions: they cannot lie outside the pretrade ratios, and they must bring desired exports and imports into equality.

Notice also that at any intermediate price ratio, both countries will completely specialize in production of the good in which it has a comparative advantage. It makes no sense for either to continue to produce a good at home that can be bought abroad at a cheaper price. More precisely, domestic production of the good in which a comparative disadvantage exists is no longer profitable, and its production ceases. In America, wine production halts; in Europe, bread production no longer takes place. This situation is depicted in Figure 1–3.

The equilibrium price ratio is indicated by the slope of the broken parallel lines. It lies between the slope of the production frontiers (and price ratios) in A and E, respectively, that are taken directly from the upper right-hand quadrant of the previous figure. We know that the new terms of trade are equilibrium ones since A's supply of exports of bread just equals E's demand for bread imports. Equivalently, A's import demand for wine is just satisfied by E's export supply at those terms of trade since both trade triangles are equal

THE GAINS FROM TRADE

Nothing in the previous analysis tells us that anybody is better off after trade than before trade. We know only: (1) that the pretrade price ratios determine the direction of comparative advantage; (2) that with constant costs of production both countries completely specialize in production at any intermediate price ratio; and (3) that trade equilibrium is brought about by terms of trade that equate desired exports and imports.

That each country realizes gains in welfare due to trade has, however, been part and parcel of trade theory since its very beginning. Not only does trade take place according to comparative advantage, but it is also a good thing. Why? Simply because by specializing in the production of goods that can be produced more cheaply at home, and exporting them for goods in which a relative disadvantage exists, more of all goods are potentially available for consumption. The proof of the gains to trade is thus very straightforward. Consider the consumption possibilities faced by America in Figure 1–3, both before and after trade. The consumption pattern D_a could not have been attained in the absence of for-

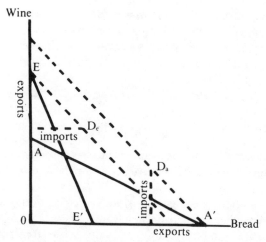

FIGURE 1–3. Trade Equilibrium. Trade equilibrium requires an exchange ratio—or terms of trade—that will simultaneously satisfy the export and import demand in both countries. The equilibrium terms of trade cannot lie outside those of America and Europe in the absence of trade; otherwise, both countries would wish to export the same good. Some intermediate price, such as indicated by the slope of the parallel, broken lines, brings into equilibrium the desired trade patterns: for example, desired exports of bread from America are just equal to the number of loaves desired by Europe, and, equivalently, the export supply and import demand for wine coincide. This is indicated by the equality of the trade triangles drawn from the points of complete specialization in wine in Europe and bread in America.

eign trade. Under autarky the maximum feasible consumption possibilities lie along the production fronter AA'. To take the simplest case, consider free trade at a constant price ratio such as the one indicated by the broken line drawn through the points A' and D_a. This means essentially that America is faced with the possibility of trading abroad without influencing foreign prices. In this instance the consumption possibilities available to America would coincide with the price line and are, therefore, everywhere superior to the consumption possibilities under self-sufficiency. For any amount of wine consumed a larger amount of bread is available for consumption. Thus no matter what the initial income distribution chosen, every single American could in principle be made better off with trade than with autarky.

A numerical example may help to clarify the gains from worldwide specialization according to the pattern of comparative advantage. Assuming the average productivity of labor data given previously, we can calculate the changes in output due to Ricardian comparative advantage. For example, suppose that in

America two workers move from the wine to the bread industry, whereas in Europe three workers move from the bread to the wine industry. The following table illustrates the change in world output as a result of greater specialization according to comparative advantage:

	America	Europe	Net Change
Wine	−50	+60	+10
Bread	+100	−90	+10

Of course, to calculate the total gains due to specialization according to comparative advantage, it would be necessary to know the sizes of the labor forces in America and Europe.

In terms of a graph (see Figure 1–4) the increased worldwide output with specialization according to comparative advantage is at point R where America completely specializes in bread and Europe in wine. Before trade each country produced some of both goods: America at point A and Europe at point E. Worldwide production before trade was thus at point S where the outputs of wine and bread from each country are added to form the parallelogram. Notice that, as illustrated, world output of both goods at R with specialization according to comparative advantage is greater than before trade at S.

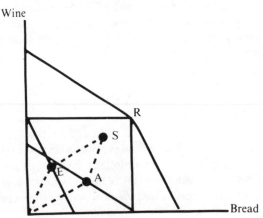

FIGURE 1–4. The Worldwide Gains from Specialization. Before trade, both countries produce some of each good. Europe produces at point E, whereas America produces at point A, so that world production is indicated by point S. After trade, Europe produces only wine and America produces only bread, which gives R, the Ricardian point of world production with specialization and trade according to comparative advantage. The Ricardian point is superior to the situation before trade.

The gains to trade for each country hold even when increased exports entail a worsening in the terms of trade. This would mean that A has some monopoly power in world markets and that the more bread A exports, the fewer bottles of wine per loaf A gets in return. In this instance the consumption possibility frontier, while bowed in one region, will still lie everywhere above the production possibility frontier AA' as illustrated in Fig. 1–5. We should note that there is one exception to the gains from trade: If American demand for wine imports were so great that it would, after trade, still need to produce some at home, it would realize no gains from trade. This would amount to making Europe a small country, as discussed in the next chapter.

TRADE AND INDIVIDUAL WELFARE

Within the simple framework of the Ricardian model, every single worker is made better off through trade than with autarky. To see that this is so, consider wages in America before and after trade. In terms of bread, a worker earns a_x loaves per period both before and after trade, the earnings reflecting the value of the individual's productivity. Because America exports bread at a higher price in terms of wine, the same number of loaves of bread earned can fetch more

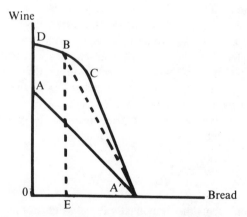

FIGURE 1–5. Trade with Some Monopoly Power. The production frontier in America is, as before, the straight line AA'. If America could trade at some constant world price, the consumption possibilities available to it with specialization in bread production and the export of bread would be everywhere superior to those attainable with self-sufficiency. Even with some monopoly power, the consumption possibilities $DBCA'$ are everywhere superior to those at autarky.

bottles of wine on the marketplace. Hence each worker enjoys a superior consumption possibility set thanks to trade. The same argument applies to a European laborer: the individual's earnings of wine are worth more loaves of bread and, accordingly, enjoys greater consumption possibilities through trade.

Note that the problem of the distribution of income within a country does not arise here: There is only one factor of production in each country, and the value of its earnings increase by trade. Suppose, however, that we temporarily depart from the technical assumptions of the Ricardian model and consider instead a world in which each individual is endowed with commodities that he or she uses to purchase other commodities. In other words we have a simple artisanlike economy. In this context some individuals are typically made better off through trade, whereas others suffer losses. To illustrate this point, let us take a simple example of a particular American that produces or has endowments of bread and wine, respectively, of X_0 and Y_0 prior to foreign trade and consumes x_0 loaves of bread and y_0 bottles of wine at the autarkic relative price of wine p_a. For this American to be neither accumulating money nor debt, the value of what he or she sells on the domestic marketplace must just cancel the value of the individual's purchases. Supposing that this person is a net consumer of bread and a net producer of wine; equilibrium in this trade position thus requires that

$$p_a (Y_0-y_0)=x_0-X_0,$$

or that sales of bread just equal purchases of wine. Now let foreign trade take place, and the new price, p_e, settles down at a different value. Since America has, by assumption, a comparative disadvantage in wine, we have $p_e<p_a$, or the price of wine has fallen. Is our arbitrarily chosen American better or worse off? Clearly, as a net producer of wine and a net consumer of bread, this person has suffered a loss in welfare; his or her wine fetches less on the marketplace—for example, bread costs the individual more. Indeed, one can measure the magnitude of his or her loss as the change in price times the net quantity traded. That is, loss can be indicated by

$$(p_a-p_e) (Y_0-y_0),$$

where (Y_0-y_0) represents the individual's initial sales of wine on the domestic market.

In short, this particular individual is made worse off owing to trade, whereas others—namely, net consumers of wine (net producers of bread)—are better off. The potential gains due to the greater possible consumption set through trade thus need not be realized by all individuals, although in principle they could be. That is, our wine producer could be bribed into accepting the trade situation, and other individuals would still be better off.

We shall return to the problem of the effect of trade upon the distribution of income in a two-factor world in Chapter 3, which focuses on the Heckscher-Ohlin trade model. Under the technical assumptions made there, trade increases the real return to the abundant factor of production and reduces the return to the scarce factor. The problem is not treated as an index one involving consumption patterns relative to commodity endowments, as in the artisan economy; rather it focuses on the link between commodity and factor prices.

In all instances, however, it is important to bear in mind that there are potential gains to be realized through trade. Stated in an alternative manner, the gains to individuals whose situation is improved exceed losses to others. This is so because with trade at any relative price pattern different from that at autarky the value of production, and hence consumption, is greater with trade than without. Since this implies that more of all commodities are potentially available to be consumed for given levels of inputs, it would be possible by an appropriate policy of income distribution for every single individual to be made better off with trade than with self-sufficiency.

RICARDO'S LAW OF PRECIOUS METALS

It is entirely conceivable that a country may initially have lower prices in terms of money of all commodities before trade. We could then say it had an absolute advantage in monetary terms in commodity trade. Take, for instance, America and Europe at the onset of trade, but let there be initial stocks of gold in each country that serve as the medium of exchange. Prior to trade, Americans and Europeans hold gold in order to separate the act of sale of wine from the act of purchase of bread; that is, gold is held as a temporary abode of purchasing power. It thereby avoids the necessity of the double coincidence of wants that must occur for pure barter trade to occur. Gold is qualitatively the same in both countries, and all prices are quoted in ounces or some equivalent unit. For any given stock of gold in either country, and with real supply and demand conditions given, there exist both a price level (some average of the bread and wine price) and a price ratio, and the latter must just equal the opportunity cost of production and consumption. It is clearly then possible for gold prices of all goods to be lower in one of the countries before trade. When trade opens up, the country with lower prices will export both bread and wine and will import, in turn, gold from the high-priced country. This means, naturally, that the first country has a surplus, whereas the second has a deficit. Consequently, gold flows from the deficit to the surplus country at an equal rate.

Can this divergence in the level of prices, and the associated flow of gold from the deficit to the surplus country, continue indefinitely? Clearly, the flow of gold will cause prices to rise in the surplus country and to fall in the deficit country in the manner of David Hume's gold-specie flow mechanism of adjustment. Gold or absolute prices of both bread and wine will quickly be brought into line in both countries so that the disequilibrium in the balance of payments and the equal gold flow will come to a halt. However, this is not all that can be said since we still have to account for relative prices, or the ratio of the absolute prices. In the absence of trade, relative prices had to conform to opportunity costs of production; otherwise, a tendency toward complete specialization arises. With trade a similar type of equilibrium must occur where the relative price at which wine and bread exchange just satisfies the export and import demand patterns. Absolute prices have to be the same; but, in addition, relative prices must adjust so as to bring the trade balance into equilibrium with no gold flows. Consequently, there is an initial period in which gold flows from the high-priced country, and wine and bread are shipped from the low-priced country. The trade pattern is, in the short run, determined by money prices and absolute advantage. However, in the final outcome the pattern of comparative advantage emerges, the gold flow stops, and trade takes place as though it were of a purely barter nature. In the previous example America would export bread and Europe would export wine even though initially one of the countries exported both in exchange for gold. This outcome has been christened *Ricardo's law of precious metals* (Ricardo 1971) and goes as follows:

> Gold and silver having been chosen for the general medium of circulation, they are, by the competition of commerce, distributed in such proportions amongst the different countries of the world as to accommodate themselves to the natural traffic which would take place if no such metals existed, and the trade between countries were purely a trade of barter. [P. 137]

Ricardo's simple proposition can explain a lot of real world phenomena. When one country has difficulty selling its products to another country, it is not because it does not have a comparative advantage; rather it is because its prices are too high. In the long run, as Ricardo argued, its absolute price level will have to fall relative to its trading partners, and two-way trade will develop. This will occur either through falling relative price and wage levels or through realignments in the exchange rate. What people really mean to say is that the United States has lost its absolute price advantage. This is certainly possible in the short run but should not be confused with the concept of comparative advantage.

Today's high-valued U.S. dollar may well be offsetting U.S. comparative advantage in some industries and accentuating foreign comparative advantage in others. For example, if $a_x/a_x^* > a_y/a_y^*$, the United States has a comparative advantage in good X. However, this comparative advantage may be temporarily offset by high U.S. money wages and/or an overvalued dollar. To see this, let w_x and w_x^* represent money wages in the United States and Europe in dollars and say francs respectively, and r be the dollar price of a franc. With only one input, labor, the cost of production of a unit of X in America and Europe, both measured in dollars, will be w_x/a_x and rw_x^*/a_x^*, respectively. This is so since $1/a_x$ and $1/a_x^*$ are the U.S. and European labor input requirements per unit of output of X. Consequently, if $w_x/a_x > rw_x^*/a_x^*$, low money wages in Europe, high money wages in the United States, and a high-priced dollar offsets comparative advantage. Equivalently, if $a_x/a_x^* < w_x/rw_x^*$, the U.S. comparative advantage is offset by a European price advantage. Since the dollar has appreciated in value a great deal relative to movements in U.S. and foreign money wages in the past three years, and is widely thought to be over-valued, it is most likely that comparative advantage has been offset in some U.S. industries recently. Or, if not offset entirely, the high exchange rate of the dollar has accentuated foreign comparative advantage, much to the distress of the U.S. textile and steel industries.

AN EMPIRICAL TEST OF THE RICARDIAN MODEL

Australian Professor R. G. D. MacDougall (1951) proposed a simple ingenious test of the Ricardian model of comparative advantage based on the pattern of British and American trade in third markets to which both countries exported in 1937. At that time, in the midst of the great 1929–39 contraction, both countries had raised tariffs in hopes of protecting domestic employment. Clearly, such beggar-my-neighbor policies may work in one country acting in isolation but must fail when all countries follow protectionism. However, since markets in third countries had the same barriers to U.S. and U.K. trade, MacDougall reasoned that the country with a true comparative advantage in a good would capture a larger share of that market. Figure 1–6 represents his attempt to correlate the ratio of U.S. to U.K. productivity of labor by industry with the ratio of U.S. exports to U.K. exports to third countries in 1937. The vertical axis plots the ratios of average productivities, a_i/a_i^*, in each industry i, whereas the horizontal axis plots the ratio of U.S. exports to U.K. exports of the same industry to third countries.

The overall picture is suggestive of a relationship: the greater the relative productivity of American labor to British labor in an industry, the greater the American share of exports in third countries. MacDougall further reasoned that the relative productivity of U.S. labor would have to be twice that of U.K. labor to offset the effect of twice-as-high money wages in the United States, as indicated by the horizontal line drawn from 2. Above this line U.S. productivity offsets high U.S. wages, whereas below it does not. Similarly, a greater U.S. share of the market is indicated by points to the right of 1 along the horizontal axis, whereas a lower share is indicated by points to the left of 1. While the simple Ricardian model does not necessarily find full jutification by this test, it is clear that the test does not reject the basic Ricardian proposition of comparative advantage.

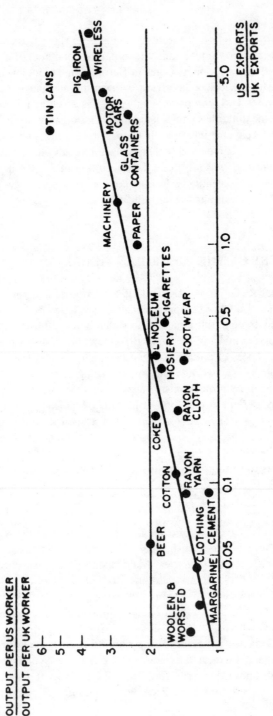

FIGURE 1–6. A Test of Ricardian Comparative Advantage. This is the MacDougall test of Ricardo's theory of comparative advantage. In 1937 a higher ratio of U.S. to British labor productivity, indicated along the vertical axis, is positively related to a higher relative share of U.S. exports to third markets. This positive relationship is consistent with the Ricardian model. (Adapted from MacDougall 1951.)

CONCLUSION

The classical trade model is as rich in policy implications as it is in tradition. The classical economists used the model to develop the principle of comparative advantage and to show that trade benefits all nations. The implications were that free trade should be promoted; and, indeed, Britain, the home of the classical economists, did pursue such a policy for most of the nineteenth century. Furthermore, even if a country were small and backward, it could expect to profit through a free trade policy.

The classical economists were also probably correct in emphasizing the importance of labor productivity in determining trade patterns. Modern theories have again returned to this interpretation, and governmental policy has recently emphasized the role of labor productivity in achieving the goals of an economic system. The pauper labor argument that low wages give an unfair advantage to foreign competition was shown to be false because national wage levels are all interdependent and determined in the long run by labor productivities. The empirical studies also indicated that labor productivities, not wage differentials, were the main determinant of the direction of trade.

The next chapter will examine alternative hypotheses to explaining trade flows and will be judged against the high standards set by the classical comparative cost theorists.

SELECTED READINGS

Balassa, Bela. 1963. "An Empirical Demonstration of Classical Comparative Cost Theory." *Review of Economics and Statistics* 45 (August).

Bhagwati, Jagdish. 1964. "The Pure Theory of International Trade: A Survey." *Economic Journal* (March): sec. 1.

Brandis, Royall. 1967. "The Myth of Absolute Advantage." *American Economic Review* (March).

Glejser, H. 1972. "Empirical Evidence on Comparative Cost Theory from the European Common Market Experience." *European Economic Review.*

Haberler, Gottfried. 1961. "A Survey of International Trade Theory." *Special Papers in International Economics,* no. 1.: International Finance Section, Princeton, N.J.: Princeton University, chap. 2.

Ingram, J. C. 1968. "The Myth of Absolute Advantage: Comment." *American Economic Review* (June).

Jones, R. 1961. "Comparative Advantage and the Theory of Tariffs: A Multi-Country, Multi-Commodity Model." *Review of Economic Studies* 28 (June).

MacDougall, R. G. D. 1951. "British and American Exports: A Study Suggested by the Theory of Comparative Costs." *Economic Journal* 61 (December).

Mill, John Stuart. 1871. *Principles of Political Economy.* London: Longmans, Green, Reader and Dyer.

Ricardo, David. 1971. *Principles of Political Economy and Taxation.* Baltimore: Penguin, chap. 7. Originally published in 1817.

Samuelson, P. 1950. ''The Gains from International Trade.'' In *Readings in the Theory of International Trade,* edited by H. S. Ellis and L. A. Metzler. Homewood, Ill.: Irwin.

TWO

APPLYING THE CLASSICAL
MODEL TO TRADE PROBLEMS

This chapter puts the Ricardian model to work on four important economic problems: the formation of customs unions—that is, preferential trading zones such as the European Common Market; differences in the size of countries; the transfer problem having to do with reparations payments, foreign aid, personal remittances, and the like; and growth and its impact on welfare at home and abroad. The Ricardian model is a very efficient workhorse, but we shall dispense with the labor theory of value embodied in it and concentrate instead on the production frontiers of America and Europe.

CUSTOMS UNION THEORY

The European Common Market, the Latin American Free Trade Area, and the North Atlantic Free Trade Area are examples of regions within which there are tariff concessions and trade preferences for members. The United States can be considered a free trade area since there are no (or rather minimal) barriers to trade between states. The theory of customs unions deals with such groupings of countries that grant members trade preferences that are not extended to nonmembers. The General Agreement on Tariffs and Trade typically outlaws tariff preferences through the most-favored-nation clause whereby any tariff concession granted by one member country to another must be extended to all member countries. However, an exemption is granted in the case of customs unions and free trade areas—in principle because there is a presumption that such preferential trading zones are a move toward freer trade for the world as a whole.

By definition, a *customs union* is a region that imposes no tariffs or quotas on trade by members but enforces a common tariff wall for nonmembers. A free trade area has no tariffs between members, but individual countries establish independent tariffs for trade with nonmembers. Obviously, with different tariffs for nonmembers, trade deflection may take place; that is, a nonmember may ship goods into a low tariff country, which are then reshipped to other member countries with no tariffs. For this reason certificates of origin are necessary. When a customs union also eliminates barriers to movements of factors of production between members, the union is called a *common market*. Perhaps the best example of a common market is the United States where there are literally no barriers to trade between states nor to movements of factors of production. Another good example of a common market is the European Economic Community.

In the theory of customs unions the two key concepts are *trade creation* and *trade diversion*. Trade creation is said to take place when a country shifts its source of supply from a high- to a low-cost source, whereas trade diversion occurs when a country shifts from a low- to a high-cost source as a result of trade preferences.

Let us take a simple example suggested by Richard Lipsey (1960). Suppose that wine can be produced in three countries—*A, B,* and *C*—at the following constant cost:

	A	B	C
Cost of wine	35	26	20

Clearly, country *C* has the worldwide comparative advantage in the production of wine. Now suppose we are citizens of country *A*, which has 100 percent tariffs. Including the tariff, wine imported from country *C* would cost 40, which is higher than the domestic price of 35. Consequently, the 100 percent tariff is prohibitive: domestic producers supply the entire domestic market in *A*. Consider now the impact of the formation of a customs union with either country *B* or *C*. If the union is with *C*, the cost of wine imported from *C* is only 20, so we shift from a high-cost domestic source of supply at 35 to a low-cost source of supply. There is thus trade creation and the presumption that the union is beneficial. Note that it is desirable that our home wine industry contract since it does not have the comparative advantage in production. If the union is with *B*, trade creation still occurs since we shift from a domestic cost of 35 to imports from B at a lower cost of 26. We do not import from *C* since the 100 percent tariff is maintained, but there is still a presumption of gain from trade creation even though it is not with the most efficient source of supply. Consequently, with high initial tariffs, there is a large, protected inefficient domestic industry that supplies at high costs; therefore, the formation of a customs union with either *B* or *C* will lead to gains according to specialization along the lines of comparative advantage.

Now consider a lower initial tariff rate of 50 percent. Country *A* will initially import wine from *C* at a tariff-inclusive price of 30 and will not produce wine at home. If *A* forms a customs union with *C*, there will not be a shifting in the source of supply, but there will be a gain in welfare since there will be a greater volume of trade. Consumers in *A* will benefit from the lower price of wine: 20 rather than 30. Suppose, on the other hand, that a union is formed with *B* instead as a partner. Clearly, *B* will now capture the market for wine from *C* because its wine exports are exempted from the tariff and thus cost only 26, whereas if *C's* wine still faces the tariff, it costs 30. This is an example of trade diversion: shifting from a low social cost source of supply (20 from *C*, since the 10 extra in tariffs is recovered by *A's* treasury) to a high social cost source of supply (26 from *B*.) The reason for this shift is that consumers take into account the price including the tariff and thus find *B's* product less expensive from a private point of view, even though it is more expensive from a social point of view. With this trade diversion there may be a loss to country *A* from joining the customs union with *B*.

To illustrate the concepts of trade creation and trade diversion graphically, let us first consider the case of country *A* with initial tariffs equal to 100 percent. In Figure 2-1 country *A's* production frontier is the line through *PA*. It displays constant opportunity costs, as in the Ricardian case. Initially, country *A* produces and consumes at point *A* since its tariffs are prohibitive to imports from *B* and *C*. Both *B* and *C* produce wine, however, at a lower opportunity cost in terms of bread. Therefore, it would be possible for country *A* to specialize completely in the production of bread at point *P* and import wine along the line

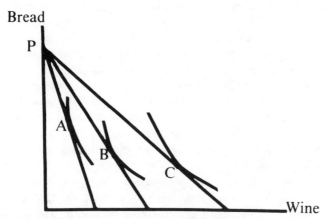

FIGURE 2-1. Trade Creation. With 100 percent tariffs America initially produces both goods at point *A*, importing no wine whatsoever. With a customs union with *C*, *A* specializes in the production of bread at *P*, imports wine from *C*, and consumes at point *C*. Welfare is increased since *A* has shifted from a high-cost domestic source of supply to a low-cost foreign source. This is called *trade creation*. Note that a customs union with *B* would also lead to trade creation, but the gains would be less because the consumption point would be at *B*.

PC from *C*, where the slope equals the price of wine in terms of bread. Or, by specializing in bread and importing from *B*, country *A* could consume along the line *PB*. Since country *C* has the worldwide comparative advantage in wine, it is clearly more advantageous to import wine from *C*.

With 100 percent tariffs, however, country *A* produces its own wine at point *A*. Now consider a customs union with country *C*. Country *A*'s production point moves to complete specialization in bread at point *P*, and consumption moves to point *C*. Country *A* now imports its wine from a low-cost source, whereas it previously obtained wine from a high-cost domestic source of production. Consequently, there is trade creation and a gain in social welfare. Similarly, had country *A* formed a customs union with *B*, *A* would specialize completely in bread at point *P* and import wine from *B*, consuming at point *B*. Once again, since country *A* shifts from a high-cost domestic source of supply to a low-cost foreign source, there is trade creation and a gain in welfare. It is clear from Figure 2-1 that the gains from a customs union with *B* are less than with *C* since *C* is the lowest-cost source of supply of wine. Nevertheless, in the case of high tariffs and consequently a closed economy, there are substantial gains to be made from trade creation.

Now consider an initial situation of 50 percent tariffs in country *A*. Initially, *A* imports wine from *C*, the country with the comparative advantage in wine. Production in Figure 2-2 takes place at a point *P* with complete specialization in bread. Consumption does not, however, take place at point *C* since there is a 50 percent tariff on imports of wine, which raises the relative price to consumers. Consequently, less wine is imported, so that the initial consumption point is at *A* where consumers equate their marginal rates of substitution in consumption to the tariff-inclusive price ratio, indicated by the slope of the line through *A* tangent to the indifference curve. This is an important point. The formation of the customs union takes place from a tariff-ridden, trade-restricted point. Now consider a customs union with country *C*. Tariffs would be removed and imports of wine from *C* would increase. The consumption point would move from *A* to *C*, and there would be a gain in welfare from expanded trade with the low-cost source of supply. This is also called *trade creation*. Thus a customs union with *C* would be beneficial.

Now consider a customs union with B. This union would involve eliminating tariffs on imports of wine from *B* but maintaining them on *C*. Country *A* would then shift its source of supply of wine from *C* to *B*. The new consumption point is at *B*, where it should be noted there is no change whatsoever in welfare compared with the tariff-ridden point *A*—despite the fact that this is an example of trade diversion.

This result may seem paradoxical, but it is not. We are not comparing free trade at point *C* with preferential trade at point *B*, but rather, tariff-restricted trade at point *A* with preferential trade at point *B*. The problem with point *A* is that the volume of trade is small, so that the gains from importing from the least-

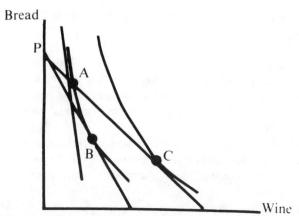

FIGURE 2-2. Trade Diversion. With 50 percent tariffs country *A* initially imports wine from *C* at the tariff-ridden point *A*. Consumers in *A* restrict their imports of wine since they equate their marginal rates of substitution in consumption to the higher tariff-inclusive price. A customs union with *C* would eliminate this tariff, trade would expand, and consumption would take place at point *C*. Consequently, there would be trade creation and gains in welfare from a customs union with *C*. A customs union with *B* would, however, involve trade diversion: a shift in the consumption point from *A* to *B*. Note that despite trade diversion there is no loss, as there is expanded trade at point *B* compared with the tariff-ridden point *A*. If the cost of wine in *B* were slightly higher, the formation of a trade-diverting customs union with *B* would entail welfare losses.

cost source of supply are restricted. With the tariff elimination on imports of wine from *B*, consumers face a lower market price and consequently expand their wine imports. This expansion in the volume of trade entails a gain in welfare that may offset the loss in welfare from shifting to a higher social cost source of supply. We owe this finding to Richard Lipsey (1960) who criticized Jacob Viner's claim that trade-diverting customs unions always entailed losses in welfare. Note that a slightly higher relative price of wine from *B* would indeed involve a lowering of welfare for *A* but that a slightly lower relative price would entail a gain in welfare for *A*, despite the presence of trade diversion. Whether or not trade diversion involves a gain or a loss in welfare depends, therefore, on the discrepancy in costs between *B* and *C*. If the difference in costs is not great, a loss in welfare to *A* will not occur. Parenthetically, U.K. resistance to joining the European Common Market involved opposition to shifting from low-cost social sources of supply of agricultural goods—Canada, Australia, and New Zealand—to high-cost social sources of European supply. This resistance to trade diversion has turned out to be well founded in light of the huge U.K. contributions to the common market's agricultural deficit, a source of Margaret Thatcher's political resistance to further agricultural deficits.

In summary, the theory of customs unions suggests the following broad propositions:

1. The more closed the economy, the greater is the likelihood of trade creation and gains from greater specialization according to comparative advantage.
2. The higher the initial level of tariffs, the greater the chance of trade creation since high-cost domestic sources of supply exist in many areas protected by high tariffs.
3. Customs unions with countries with whom much trade already takes place are likely to involve mainly trade creation since it is presumably the most efficient worldwide source of supply that has the market since all countries face the same tariffs.
4. Countries that produce many of the same types of goods stand to gain from formation of customs unions since the most efficient supplier captures the market. Hence there is trade creation thanks to greater specialization according to comparative advantage within the union.

COUNTRY SIZE AND THE DISTRIBUTION OF THE GAINS FROM TRADE

There is an interesting proposition regarding the relative sizes of countries and the distribution of the gains from trade: Small countries tend to gain relative to large ones as a result of trade.

Consider a situation in which, when trade opens up, the demand for imports in one country exceeds the supply of exports from the other at any price ratio between the pretrade ratios. This would imply that demand in one country was so large that imports of the good in which it has a comparative disadvantage would never be sufficient to satisfy domestic demand fully. Home production of the import good would still have to take place. This country, *defined* in this way as the large one, would not completely specialize in production; and for this reason the posttrade price ratio would be the same as in the large country before trade. The small country, whose export supplies fail to satisfy foreign demand fully, will, on the other hand, completely specialize in the production of its export good and will simply trade at the foreign price ratio. Hence its exports serve only to displace production in the large country partially. In the large country the consumption possibilities with trade are no different than those without trade because prices are unchanged, whereas in the small country complete specialization takes place and the opportunity to trade at the large country's price ratio affords a greater consumption possibility set than before trade. In short, the small country gains from trade, whereas there is no change in welfare in the large one. We should be careful to remember that *size* is defined in this context in terms of an excess demand for imports by the large country at any price ratio between those that would reign at autarky and is not necessarily related to the population sizes of the countries. This point will be taken up again later; first, let us have a look at the argument graphically (see Figure 2-3).

America is the large country. At any price of bread slightly lower than its price at self-sufficiency, AA', it would tend to specialize completely in bread production and demand imports of wine near the amount indicated by D_A. Not only could Europe, the small country, fail to satisfy this demand if it produced only wine and exported all of it; in addition, its export supplies would fall short of American demand at any price ratio near AA' since some wine is consumed at home. And strictly speaking, it is this latter condition that makes for the notion of size. Following trade, Europe adopts the American price, AA', so its consumption possibilities along ER are everywhere superior to those attainable by self-sufficiency, EE'. Europe completely specializes in the production of wine

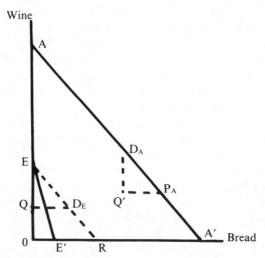

FIGURE 2-3. The Problem of Country Size. At any relative price of bread slightly higher than the autarkic one AA', America would completely specialize in the production of bread. However, Europe neither could nor would wish to supply the quantity of wine imports demanded; so as a result America must continue to produce some wine at home after trade. Consequently, the world terms of trade remain equal to those in America before trade, and the demand pattern in America remains at D_A. Europe completely specializes in wine production at E, exporting EQ bottles in exchange for QD_E loaves of bread. Wine production in America is thus displaced by the same amount, D_AQ', and its production of bread rises by the number of loaves exported, P_AQ'. The large country, America, specializes only partially and gains nothing from trade with the small country, Europe. However, Europe has a superior consumption possibility set ORE as a result of trading at America's price ratio.

producing OE loaves, exports EQ of them, and imports QD_E loaves of bread. In America the demand pattern, D_A, is unchanged by trade because the price ratio remains the same. The supply pattern, initially D_A also, is slightly displaced to P_A by trade since imports of wine equal to D_AQ' ($=EQ$) take place, and exports of $Q'P_A$ ($=QD_E$) loaves of bread are made. Trade balances owing to the fact that demand for imports just cancels in value at the price ratio AA'—for example, the trade triangles are equal. The small country enjoys *all* the gains to trade.

This proposition can be extended to allow for greater relative gains to trade by small countries since they, by definition, tend to adopt prices nearer those that would reign in large countries in the absence of trade.

So we have an exception to the Ricardian rules that (1) countries tend to specialize completely after trade and (2) that all countries tend to realize gains in welfare owing to the existence of trade. The exception, however, is a subtle one that bears closer examination. In the first place the population size of a country need not coincide with the definition of *country size* that we have just outlined. To see that this is so, consider the following experiment. Suppose that the ratios of the average productivities of labor were exactly the same in America and Europe. In the absence of trade, relative prices would then be identical in both countries, no matter what the population size of either country. We could double, triple, or quadruple the number of inhabitants in either country, and yet the relative prices would remain the same. Would trade take place? Clearly not, because neither country has a comparative advantage in either good. The possibility of trade would be an irrelevant opportunity since each country could do just as well by remaining self-sufficient. Graphically, the production possibility frontiers would have the same slopes and would be shifted proportionally outward with an increase in population size. No matter how great the difference in population sizes, trade does not take place when opportunity costs are the same in both countries. We may conclude then that if we keep all other factors constant—in particular, techniques of production—varying solely the relative population sizes plays absolutely no role because trade does not take place.

What, however, if the opportunity costs of production in the two countries differ but are constant as in the Ricardian model? Is there then a relationship between population size and the notion of relative country size that we have associated with supply and demand conditions? In this case we can easily see that varying the population size (which we are identifying here with the size of the labor force) does have the effect of increasing the demand for both goods at the initial domestic price ratios. Clearly, we can keep the population size of one country constant while increasing the population of the other so as to increase the demand for imports in the country with a growing population. It takes only an instant to realize that no matter what the difference in opportunity costs of production, there is now some crucial population size in America for any given population in Europe that will make America's demand for imports so large that following trade it will continue to produce both goods.

To summarize, then, we have seen that with equal opportunity costs varying solely the relative population sizes has no effect since trade is irrelevant. If opportunity costs differ, however, enlarging the population of one country relative to the other will have the effect of making the country with a growing population larger in the economic sense of increasing its demand for imports at the initial domestic price ratio. Similarly, diminishing a country's population would have the effect of reducing its export supply at the autarkic price ratio, thereby making it a smaller country in the economic sense.

For the next two problems that we take up, transfers and growth, we will take a Ricardian case of trade in which both America and Europe completely specialize in the good in which they have a comparative advantage: that is, wine and bread, respectively. We will, in short, put aside for the moment the problem of size and incomplete specialization. The main difference that arises due to the assumption of complete specialization is that domestic production does not typically vary following changes in the relative price of the goods. Rather, both countries remain completely specialized throughout. For most problems this entails little loss in generality. When the loss is considerable, we will take pains to point out its implications.

THE TRANSFER PROBLEM

Suppose that, for one reason or another, America transfers some of its bread to Europe, not in exchange for goods but rather much like a gift. War reparations payments, guest worker remittances, and foreign aid are examples of such transfers. The payment is in the form of a shipment of bread that like any other type of income must come from somewhere. To simplify, we assume that America taxes its citizens to raise the revenue and that the recipient country, Europe, distributes the proceeds directly to its citizens. Ignoring any impact on the terms of trade, the transfer of income has the immediate consequence of reducing income and consequently consumption in America and increasing income and consumption in Europe. Such changes in the demand pattern at constant terms of trade, however, create a trade imbalance, which in turn must be eliminated by a change in the terms of trade. The secondary welfare effects of the change in the terms of trade have come to be called the *transfer problem*, and the question is whether welfare in America falls by more or less than that entailed by the pure transfer itself. If the price of bread falls, America suffers more than the strict burden of the transfer. Equivalently, an improvement in Europe's terms of trade would have the effect of increasing income by more than the transfer. The natural question is, What does the change in the terms of trade hinge upon?

First, the transfer causes an equal fall in income in America and an equal rise in income in Europe. With changes in income the demand patterns in each country cannot remain the same. In particular, demand for imports of bread in Europe will rise by some proportion m_e, whereas the supply of exports of bread from America will rise by a proportion c_a of the transfer. This results since the increased income in Europe is partly spent on bread, whereas the reduced income in America causes a fall in expenditure on bread, thereby releasing extra supplies of bread from domestic consumption. With equal changes in income we need only ask whether the proportional rise in demand for imports of bread in Europe exceeds, equals, or falls short of the *rise* in supply of bread exports in America. If the transfer causes an excess demand for bread ($m_e > c_a$), Europe runs into a deficit, and the price of bread must rise to bring about a new equilibrium. If the transfer causes a deficit for America ($m_e < c_a$), the price of bread falls. And the borderline case with no change in the balance of trade nor in its terms involves $m_e = c_a$.

But these terms have familiar names: m_e is Europe's marginal propensity to import bread out of extra income, and c_a is America's marginal propensity to consume home goods. Hence the transferring country's terms of trade improve, worsen, or remain unchanged depending upon whether the recipient country's marginal propensity to import exceeds, falls short of, or equals the marginal propensity to consume home goods in the transferring country. We can express this condition in a similar fashion. Letting m_a represent America's marginal propensity to import wine, and assuming that all extra income is spent, we have $c_a + m_a = 1$, or the sum of the marginal propensities to consume equal unity. Thus, if $m_e < c_a$, then $m_a + m_e < 1$, which is the familiar *transfer criterion*: If the sum of the marginal propensities to import is less than one, the transferring country suffers a secondary transfer burden due to the worsening of the terms of trade necessary to eliminate the deficit caused by the transfer. (See Figure 2–4.)

The initial production points in America and Europe are, respectively, A' and E with complete specialization, and the consumption points are Q' in America and Q in Europe. Trade is in balance at the terms AA' or EE', and the value of consumption in each country equals the value of production. With a transfer of $Q'S'$ loaves of bread, however, the value of income after taxes falls by $Q'S'$ in America, whereas it rises by the equivalent amount QS in Europe. As a result, demand in America falls to point T', whereas it rises to T in Europe. Consequently, the supply of bread exports from America rises by $Q'R'$, whereas the demand for bread imports rises by QR in Europe. Should the length of the two segments be equal, the equilibrium would be undisturbed and the terms of trade AA' and EE' would remain the same. Since the value of the changes in income are equal to the transfer, the proportional rise in the supply of exports from America, $Q'R'/Q'S'$, and the proportional rise in the demand for imports in Europe, QR/QS, are defined as the marginal propensity to consume home goods

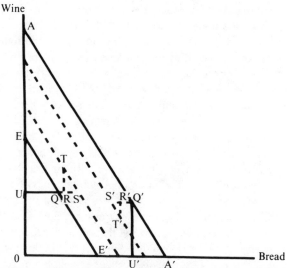

FIGURE 2–4. America Transfers Income to Europe. At the outset, trade is in balance since the trade triangles *EUQ* and *A'U'Q'* are equal, signifying equality of supply and demand for imports, with each country specializing in the good in which it has a comparative advantage. At the initial terms of trade, *AA'* and *EE'*, the market values of production in Europe and America, respectively, are *OE* and *OA* bottles of wine and or *OE'* and *OA'* loaves of bread. America transfers *Q'S'* loaves of bread to Europe. As a result, the value of consumption in America falls by the same amount whereas in Europe it rises by the same amount *QS*. However, the demand patterns need not change in an identical way. In America the demand for bread falls by *Q'R'*, whereas it rises by QR in Europe. Thus, if *Q'R'* is greater than *QR*, there results an excess supply of bread and its price must fall. Equivalently, if *QR/QS* is less than *Q'R'/Q'S'*, the transferring country suffers a secondary burden in the worsening of its terms of trade. In technical terms, if the recipient country's marginal propensity to import is less than the transferring country's marginal propensity to consume home goods, the terms of trade move against the transferring country.

in America, c_a, and the marginal propensity to import in Europe, m_e. This information, in turn, gives us the criterion developed verbally for the direction of the change in the terms of trade. If $c_a > m_a$, America suffers a secondary burden from the transfer via a worsening in the terms of trade.

Economic Growth

With complete specialization, growth involves simply an increase in the productivity of the factors of production—more bread can, for example, be produced by America. We can break down the problem into two parts: (1) the impact of growth on the trade balance and (2) the change in the terms of trade necessary to eliminate any resulting disequilibrium. A rise in productivity alone means an increase in the output of bread at constant terms of trade. What happens to the extra loaves of bread? As with an increase in income, some of it will be demanded at home, and the remainder will serve to increase the supply of bread exports. If we analyze the impact on America's trade balance, import demand for bread will increase by the U.S. marginal propensity to import, m_a, times the increase in bread production, dX. If Europe fails to grow along with America, the supply of wine exports remains unchanged; and as a consequence America's deficit of $m_a dX$ sets into motion the familiar price mechanism that serves to eliminate the deficit. The price of America's export good must fall, each loaf of bread commanding fewer bottles of wine on the world market.

We know that growth alone has the effect of increasing welfare and that by itself a worsening of the terms of trade has the effect of reducing welfare. An interesting question now arises: Could the deterioration in the terms of trade be so severe that American welfare actually declines despite the increase in productivity? Curiously enough, such immiserizing growth where the country ends up worse off is a possibility. To make things simple, let us first see how we could rule out immiserizing growth. If the extra export of bread is accompanied by an increased import of wine, American welfare cannot fall. Why not? Because part of the increased production of bread is consumed at home, and with increased imports of wine the consumption of both commodities is greater. Using this criterion as a measure of (potential) welfare, we must say that America is better off if its extra export of bread fetches more wine on the world marketplace.

This condition can be expressed in terms of elasticities: If the European supply of wine rises with the enlarged demand in America, the latter's welfare must increase. In short, if the foreign elasticity of export supply is positive, growth at home cannot be immiserizing. Notice that this means, equivalently, that European demand for imports of bread is elastic (exceeds unity) since the increased export supply of American bread causes an increased wine revenue. Clearly, then, a necessary condition for immiserizing growth with complete specialization is that the foreign demand for the home country's exports be inelastic. This is not a sufficient condition, however, because the reduced imports of wine might well have a smaller impact on welfare than the increased consumption of bread. That is, we cannot a priori state that growth is immiserizing if foreign demand is inelastic: while there is less of the import good available for consumption, the export good is more abundant. A sufficient condition for impoverishing growth must therefore require that the value of the reduction in consumption of the one good exceed the value of the increase in consumption of the other.

Before turning to the graphical exposition of the argument, we might stress a few points. First, real income in Europe, the country that is not growing, rises as a result of the improved price of its export good. In a sense part of the growth in productivity in America has been exported abroad. Second, since the feedback impact on American welfare hinges upon an increased price of the import good, if that good could be produced at home at constant costs, the domestic import-competing industry would simply expand, thereby barring any worsening in the terms of trade. In general, therefore, the greater the ease of domestic import substitution, the less the worsening of the terms of trade. Consequently, incomplete specialization and ease of shuffling resources into the domestic import-competing industry provide for a safeguard from the secondary welfare effects of possible deterioration in the terms of trade. Third, with incomplete specialization, it is entirely possible that growth takes place relatively faster in the import-competing industry, thereby causing a surplus, and not a deficit, in the growing country's trade balance. As a result the increase in real income need not be less than the increase in productivity; instead, it would be greater owing to the improvement in the terms of trade. Fourth, if the European supply of wine exports declines with an increase in price, as is necessary for American growth to be immiserizing, America could adopt the policy of raising tariffs, thereby curbing the demand for wine imports but also increasing the number of bottles imported. As long as the supply curve is negatively sloped, it would pay America to raise tariffs. With such a policy, growth could never be immiserizing since the tariff policy just outlined would move American import demand into a positively sloped region of Europe's supply curve.

We will not take up these problems in greater detail. The graphical exposition of immiserizing growth in that framework is simple enough. Examine Figure 2-5.

Initially, America's production of bread is OP loaves, whereas the consumption pattern is characterized by point C. The terms of trade are the slope of the line CP. Following an increase in productivity of PP' loaves per period, the price of bread falls on the world market—as indicated by the less steep slope of the line $C'P'$, where C' is the new consumption point, and P' is the new production point. Equivalently, wine is now more expensive. Notice, however, that wine imports have fallen at C' over the initial consumption pattern C. Europe must therefore be exporting fewer bottles at the higher price, implying a negative export supply elasticity if the point C' is indeed one of equilibrium. By drawing an indifference curve passing through both consumption points, we illustrate a case where America neither gains nor loses owing to the increase in productivity. The fall in the price of bread has just offset the value of the increased productivity.

CONCLUSION

This chapter has put the Ricardian model to work to shed light on a number of important international problems. First, whether or not a country gains

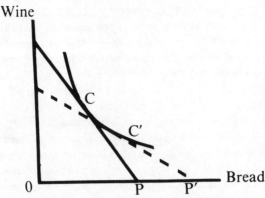

FIGURE 2-5. Immiserizing Growth. Initially, America completely specializes in the production of bread at P, part of which is exported in order to consume some wine at C. Owing to technical progress, America's production of bread rises to OP', but the world market price falls so much that at the new consumption pattern C' America is no better off than before growth. Since the new consumption point involves fewer imports of wine at the higher price, this implies that the world demand for bread was inelastic, or equivalently that the foreign supply curve of wine was negatively sloped. Had the world price of America's export good fallen slightly more, the United States would have suffered a loss in welfare.

from joining a customs union will depend on the extent of trade creation—shifting to a low-cost source of supply—relative to trade diversion—shifting to a high-cost source of supply. In general, countries with high initial tariffs and a small international trade sector will clearly gain from the formation of customs unions with countries with whom they already trade a great deal. Second, the Ricardian model shows that small countries benefit more from trade thanks to a greater degree of specialization according to comparative advantage. This suggests that protectionist policies are more costly in small countries. Third, when one country transfers income to another, there is a presumption of a secondary lowering in welfare as a result of a deterioration in the transferring country's terms of trade. This further decline in welfare results since the recipient country is presumed to spend less of the transfer on the transferring country's goods than would have been spent in the transferring country. Finally, in the Ricardian model growth is export-intensive and hence worsens the home country's terms of trade. In a special case, growth can actually be immiserizing.

SELECTED READINGS

Balassa, B. 1975. *European Economic Integration*. Amsterdam: North-Holland.
Bhagwati, Jagdish. 1958. "Immiserizing Growth: A Geometrical Note." *Review of Economic Studies* (June).

Corden, W. M. 1972. "Economies of Scale and Customs Union Theory." *Journal of Political Economy* (March).

Findlay, Ronald, and H. Grubert. 1969. "Factor Intensities, Technological Progress and the Terms of Trade." *Oxford Economic Papers* (February).

Johnson, Harry. 1955. "The Transfer Problem: A Note on Criteria for Changes in the Terms of Trade." *Economics* (May).

——. 1962. "Economic Development and International Trade." *Money, Trade, and Economic Growth*. Cambridge, Mass.: Harvard University Press, chap. 4.

Krauss, Melvyn B. 1972. "Recent Developments in Customs Union Theory: An Interpretative Survey." *Journal of Economic Literature* 10 (June).

Lipsey, Richard G. 1960. "The Theory of Customs Unions: A General Survey." *Economic Journal* 70 (September).

Mundell, Robert. 1960. "The Pure Theory of International Trade." *American Economic Review* (March).

Samuelson, Paul. 1952. "The Transfer Problem and Transport Costs: I, The Terms of Trade When Impediments Are Absent." *Economic Journal*, June.

——. 1954. "The Transfer Problem and Transport Costs: Analysis of Effects of Trade Impediments." *Economic Journal* (June).

Viner, Jacob. 1950. *The Customs Union Issue*. New York: Carnegie Foundation for International Peace.

THREE

THE HECKSCHER-OHLIN TRADE MODEL

In the Ricardian model the source of comparative advantage lies in the differences in productivities and techniques of production. Further, labor, the sole factor of production, gains unambiguously from trade. By contrast, in the Heckscher-Ohlin model techniques of production are the same everywhere; so it is the relative abundance of factors of production that determines the pattern of comparative advantage. In particular, if a country is abundantly endowed with capital relative to other countries, it will have a comparative advantage in capital-intensive goods. Exporting capital goods favors capital and harms labor by raising rents and lowering real wages. That is, one factor of production, the abundant one, benefits from trade, whereas the other, the scarce one, is harmed by trade. This chapter develops the Heckscher-Ohlin model in detail and discusses the famous empirical test of this model for the United States by Wassily Leontief (1954), a test now known as the Leontief paradox.

The Heckscher-Ohlin trade model bears the name of its originators: Eli Heckscher first presented the theory in 1919, and Bertil Ohlin elaborated upon it in 1933 in his *Interregional and International Trade*. It was further developed by modern writers, most notably by Paul Samuelson (1949) in a number of articles that explore in detail the impact of foreign trade on returns to factors of production. The particular advantage of the Heckscher-Ohlin model is that it provides a clear picture of the workings of factor markets in a relatively simple framework, allowing for a theory of comparative advantage that is not based on differences in technology, as in the Ricardian model. Another distinguishing feature of the Heckscher-Ohlin model is the rigid link made between foreign trade and the domestic distribution of income among factors. As shall become clear, a central feature of the model is the role played by the factor endowments of the respective economies.

TECHNIQUES OF PRODUCTION

We assume two factors of production, capital and labor, whose supplies are fixed. The factors are qualitatively identical between the two countries, and they are perfectly mobile within the same country but do not move at all between countries. Only two commodities are produced, bread and wine. Further, the technological production functions are assumed (1) to be the same in the two countries, (2) to display constant returns to scale (that is, changing all inputs in the same proportion changes output in the same proportion), and (3) to have diminishing marginal productivity for each factor. This means that the marginal product of a factor diminishes as more of that factor is used, holding other factors constant. Finally, one of the goods, say wine, is assumed to be labor-intensive relative to bread for each and every factor price ratio. In other words the wine industry has a higher labor-capital ratio than the bread industry at every factor price ratio.

The assumptions above are sufficient to enable us to describe the production possibilities of each of the economies. In Figure 3–1 we have a familiar Edgeworth-Bowley box diagram where the lengths of the sides represent for the particular economy in question the total endowments of capital and labor, respectively.

Any point within the factor box represents a particular allocation of the factors of production between the wine and bread industries, the origins of which diagonally oppose each other. The maximum amount of wine producible for any arbitrarily selected level of output of bread, X_0, is obtained when the marginal rates of substitution between capital and labor are equal, as depicted by the tangency of the isoquants at point P. The locus of points satisfying the efficiency condition is drawn in the figure and lies everywhere above the labor-capital endowment ratio (the slope of the diagonal) since wine is the labor-intensive commodity. With perfectly competitive behavior on all markets, as assumed here, a point on the efficiency locus such as P will be reached.

Along any straight line emanating from the wine origin, the labor-capital ratio is constant. As a result of our technical assumptions, we can make the following statements regarding wine isoquants that share a common factor ratio, or lie along the same line from the origin:

1. The marginal products of capital and labor remain constant.
2. The marginal rate of substitution between labor and capital is the same.
3. Output is proportional to the distance from the origin to each isoquant; for example, an isoquant lying twice as far from the origin on the same line is associated with twice as much output.
4. The isoquants are convex from their origin.

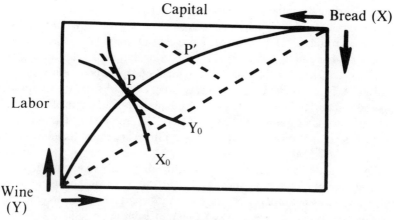

FIGURE 3-1. **Factor Endowment Box.** The lengths of the sides of the factor endowment box represent the labor and capital endowments of the country. Any point within the box represents a particular allocation of factors between the wine industry, whose origin is in the southwest corner, and the bread industry, whose origin is in the northeast corner. Efficient factor allocation requires that the marginal rates of factor substitution (the slopes of the isoquants X_0 and Y_0) be equal with full employment of both factors, such as at point P. With constant returns to scale, and diminishing marginal productivities, one of the commodities (wine) can be identified as the labor-intensive good. As output of that good expands, for example, from P to P', the labor-capital ratio declines in both industries, causing a higher relative and real return (marginal product) to labor and a lower relative and real return to capital. Consequently, if the country has a comparative advantage in wine, trade will favor labor and harm capital.

Constant returns to scale means that the production functions are homogeneous of degree one, or $\lambda X = X(\lambda L, \lambda K)$. That is, multiplying employment of all factors by the same (positive) number λ results in an equal change in output. Let $\lambda = 1/K$; then $X = KX(L/K, 1)$, or $X = Kx(L/K)$. Consequently,

$$\frac{\partial X}{\partial K} = x - (L/K)x'$$

and

$$\partial X / \partial L = x'.$$

In short, the marginal products of labor and capital depend solely upon the labor-capital ratio. This confirms statement 1. Since the marginal rate of substitution between labor and capital is the ratio of the marginal product of capital to the marginal product of labor, and these are constant along the same line, statement 2 follows immediately. Furthermore, since constant returns to scale means that for a given labor-capital ratio output is proportional to the level of input of capital, or $X=Kx(L/K)$, and since the level of input of capital is measured along the horizontal axis, proportionate movements along any line from the origin imply proportionate movements in output. For example, a point lying half the distance between the wine origin and the point P along the line joining the two has exactly half the output of wine as at P. This confirms statement 3 and is very important for later analysis.

Finally, as the labor-capital ratio falls, the marginal product of labor rises, and the marginal product of capital falls. This follows from the assumption of diminishing marginal productivity together with constant returns to scale. Consequently, the isoquants are convex as viewed from the origin.

TRADE AND REAL WAGES

As the wine industry expands along the efficiency locus at the expense of the bread industry, the labor-capital ratio declines in both industries. This can be verified by comparing the slope of a line from the wine origin to a point northeast of P such as P' and the slope of a line from P' to the bread origin. Thus, as the labor-intensive industry expands, the labor-capital ratio falls in both industries. Consequently, the marginal product of labor rises, whereas that of capital falls. We can conclude that an expansion in a particular industry has the effect of driving up the real wage of the factor intensive to that industry and driving down the real wage of the other. This implies, in addition, a less steep slope of the relative factor price line passing through P'. Intuitively, the expansion of a particular industry causes an excess demand for the factor it uses intensively, thereby bidding up its price. Equivalently, an excess supply of the other factor is created, thereby driving down its price. As a result neither industry can expand at constant costs, despite the presence of constant returns to scale. This implies that the transformation curve is concave to the origin—or displays increasing opportunity costs of production—and that higher relative prices of wine imply higher relative and absolute wages of labor and lower relative and absolute returns to capital.

We may now move directly to the proposition that trade has the effect of increasing the real wage of the factor intensive to the good in which the country has a comparative advantage and lowering the real wage of the other factor. This results because the posttrade price of the good in which the country has a comparative advantage will be higher, thereby inducing an expansion in that industry and a redistribution of income in favor of the factor intensive to the export industry. The argument can be verified by comparing points P and P' in Figure 3-1. This is the Stolper-Samuelson (1941) proof.

Notice that we have simply assumed that the country in question has a comparative advantage in wine, without bothering to explain the source of comparative advantage. This is the next step in the analysis. The basic Heckscher-Ohlin proposition is that each country will have a comparative advantage in the good that uses its relatively abundant factor intensively.

THE HECKSCHER-OHLIN THEOREM

In the Heckscher-Ohlin model the pattern of comparative advantage (ignoring complications on the demand side) is determined solely by the relative endowments of the factors of production. The Heckscher-Ohlin theorem goes as follows: Each country will have a comparative advantage in the good that uses its abundant factor intensively. Thus, if capital is abundant in America while labor is abundant in Europe, America will have a comparative advantage in bread, the capital-intensive good, whereas Europe will have a comparative advantage in wine, the labor-intensive good. The Heckscher-Ohlin theorem is demonstrated in two steps: first, making use of the theorem of proportions and, then, calling upon the Rybczynski theorem.

The Theorem of Proportions

Consider a particular economy with given endowments of the factors of production and take any given production pattern and associated resource allocation. Now change the endowment of each factor proportionately, so that the total labor-capital ratio of the economy is unchanged. Then, at constant commodity and factor prices, the outputs of the two goods will change in the exact same proportion.

In Figure 3-2a, point A is the initial resource allocation, and point P of Figure 3-2b is the corresponding initial production pattern. Now increase the sides of the factor box proportionately, holding the endowment ratio constant. For commodity and factor prices to remain unchanged, the labor-capital ratios of each industry must remain the same. This is so because the ratio of the marginal products depends solely upon the industry factor intensities. Consequently, point B is the new resource allocation with unchanged factor ratios. The proportional change in the output of wine is AB/OA or CD/OA, and the proportional change in the output of bread is DE/BD or DE/AC. Since the two triangles OAC and CDE are similar by equal angles, production of bread and wine rise by the same proportion. Furthermore, since the proportionate increase in the factor endowments can be measured by CE/OC, the ratio of the bases of the similar trian-

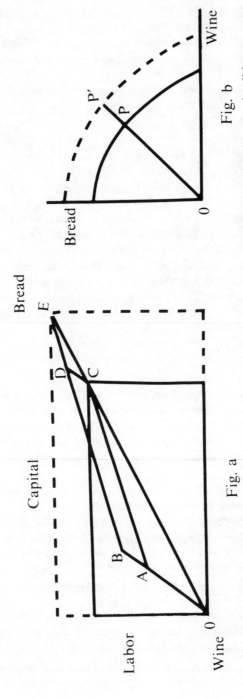

Fig. a

Fig. b

FIGURE 3-2. **Theorem of Proportions.** With constant returns to scale an equiproportionate increase in all inputs causes an equiproportionate increase in all outputs at constant prices. Departing from point *A* in Figure 3–2*a*, the proportionate increases in the factor endowment and the outputs of wine and bread are, respectively, *CE*/*OC*, *CD*/*OA*, and *DE*/*AC*. Since the triangles *OAC* and *CDE* are similar owing to equal angles, all factors and outputs change in the same proportion. This equiproportionate outward shift in the production frontier is depicted in Figure 3–2*b*.

gles, the change in outputs is proportionate to the change in inputs. In short, the production frontier in Figure 3-2b shifts outward in the same proportion PP'/OP, keeping the same slope or opportunity cost for each wine-bread ratio. So, the scale of outputs is proportionate to the scale of inputs. If the demand pattern also depended only upon the proportions in which the commodities are consumed, the points P and P' would, for instance, be equilibrium points for a closed economy. The relative price of the goods would thus depend only upon their relative outputs.

The Rybczynski Theorem

To complete the proof of the determination of the pattern of comparative advantage, we can make use of what is known as the Rybczynski theorem: At constant commodity prices an increase in the endowment of one factor—the quantity of the other held constant—causes an expansion in the production of the commodity that uses that factor intensively and a contraction in the output of the other commodity. For instance, if the labor force increases in size, the output of wine will rise and that of bread will fall at the initial commodity price ratio. The proposition makes sense intuitively: If the supply of labor increases, this would tend to cheapen the production of wine relative to bread. To nullify any fall in the price of wine, wine production must rise and bread production must fall to take up the excess supply of labor at the initial factor and commodity prices. The point can be made geometrically.

If the commodity price ratio is to be held constant, owing to the one-to-one relationship between commodity and factor prices, then so must the factor price ratio. The factor price ratio equals the marginal rate of substitution between the factors at Q (the slopes of the isoquants). Consequently, following an increase in the labor supply of ΔL, the factor use ratios in each industry must remain the same to keep the factor price ratio unchanged. Thus, if Q is the initial resource allocation, the new one with the same factor price ratios must be at Q' in Figure 3–3a. But this implies that output of the wine industry has expanded, whereas output in the bread industry has contracted, as measured by the lengths from the origins to the points Q and Q'. What this means is that the production frontier will shift outward in a biased way in favor of the wine industry at a given relative price, as depicted by the points P and P' in Figure 3–3b.

Now suppose that the two transformation curves in Figure 3–3b represent the two countries, with Europe having the larger endowment of labor. In addition, assume that the indifference curves summarizing the taste patterns of the two countries are identical, convex, and that their slopes depend solely upon the ratios in which the two goods are consumed. In technical terms the indifference curves are *homothetic*. In the absence of trade Europe would have a lower relative price of wine than America. For example, at autarky the production pattern in America might be at P, and the production pattern in Europe at point R.

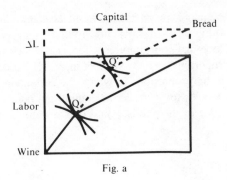

Fig. a

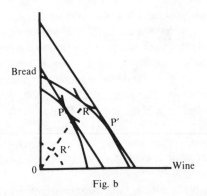

Fig. b

FIGURE 3-3. The Rybczynski Theorem. At constant commodity and factor prices an increase in the endowment of one factor, the quantity of the other held constant, causes the output of the good that uses the increased factor intensively to rise and the output of the good that uses the other factor intensively to decline. In Figure 3-3a the increase in the labor endowment is ΔL. Factor and commodity prices are equal at points Q and Q'; hence output of the wine industry has expanded and that of the bread industry has contracted (as measured along the segments from the origins). Figure 3-3b depicts this biased shift in the production frontier, where the initial production point is P and the new one is P' at the same relative price. If we now suppose that the two production frontiers correspond to two different countries with identical and homothetic indifference patterns, the country with the increased labor endowment would have a lower relative price of wine at R compared with P and, consequently, a comparative advantage in wine. In fact, as long as that country has a higher labor-capital endowment ratio, it will—under these assumptions— have a comparative advantage in wine. For instance, the same relative price of wine prevails at R' as at R with all outputs and endowments being reduced proportionately. This is the Heckscher-Ohlin theorem; the pattern of comparative advantage is determined by relative factor endowments.

A lower ratio of bread to wine is consumed in Europe, and the relative price (equal to the slope of the frontiers at P and R) of wine is cheaper in Europe. In short, with identical tastes and homothetic indifference curves, the labor-abundant country has a comparative advantage in wine, the good that uses labor intensively.

Notice, however, that the proof is not as yet perfectly general. We have chosen a case in which the capital endowments of the two countries are the same, whereas the labor endowment of one country exceeds that of the other. The Heckscher-Ohlin theorem has to do with relative factor abundancy—that is, solely the endowment ratios. To make the argument perfectly general, we can keep the same labor-capital endowment ratio in Europe but vary all factors in the same proportion, for example, by shrinking Europe in Figure 3-3b. The production frontier is moved proportionately toward the origin. Note, however, that the price will remain the same at R' as at R. This is so because the production frontier has the same slope at the two points and, further, so do the relevant indifference curves. Thus, independently of size, Europe will have a comparative advantage in wine so long as Europe's labor-capital ratio exceeds America's.

In conclusion, we might stress the importance of the demand conditions that had to be introduced to validate the Heckscher-Ohlin theorem. The indifference curves are identical, and their slopes depend upon the proportions in which the goods are consumed. Were this not the case, differences in the demand pattern could reverse Europe's comparative advantage in wine. For instance, Europe may have a marked preference for wine sufficient to make its price higher than in America at autarky, despite the relative abundance of labor in Europe. The taste pattern could offset the relative production efficiencies.

FACTOR PRICE EQUALIZATION

If, in addition to the assumptions made above, we suppose that there are no tariffs, transport costs, or other impediments to trade and that both countries continue to produce both goods following trade, real factor prices are equalized in America and Europe by trade. This is Paul Samuelson's (1949) celebrated factor price equalization theorem. Essentially, it means that trade is a perfect substitute for factor mobility. Its proof runs as follows: With identical production functions, constant returns to scale, and diminishing marginal productivities, there is an identical one-to-one relationship between relative commodity and relative factor prices in each country. In particular, higher relative prices of wine are associated with higher relative prices of labor, the factor intensive to the wine industry. Free trade equalizes relative commodity prices and, consequently, relative factor prices. However, if relative factor prices are the same, then so must be the labor-capital ratios of the respective industries in each country. This is so because the marginal rates of factor substitution depend only upon the capital-labor ratios. Further, with identical factor-use ratios, the marginal products of labor and capital (or real returns measured in either commodity) will be the same in both countries. Figure 3–4 depicts this situation.

Equality of relative commodity and relative factor prices is satisfied at point P and P' since the slopes of the isoquants are parallel. Some of both commodities are produced in both countries. The factor proportions in the wine industries and the bread industries are identical, as are the real returns to the factors (the marginal products) because the production functions are identical and display constant returns to scale. (Recall that with constant returns to scale the marginal products depend only on the labor-capital ratio.) We should note, in conclusion, that if complete specialization occurred in either of the countries as a result of trade, there would be a tendency toward factor price equalization, although incomplete.

TRADE AND UNEMPLOYMENT

We have previously seen in the context of the Heckscher-Ohlin trade model that the real wage of the scarce factor falls as a result of trade, whereas the real return of the abundant factor rises. This is the Stolper-Samuelson result: Trade and income distribution are intimately linked. What would happen, however, if, after a point, in part the real wage of the scarce factor were rigid downward? Could trade not lead to unemployment and in part to a lowering of real wages in this industry and, consequently, to losses from trade? This is entirely possible. In Figure 3–5 the autarkic input point in the production box is indicated by P. With trade an expansion in the production of bread and a contraction in the production of wine would occur at point R, which corresponds to a lower capital-labor ratio in both industries. This means lower real wages of labor in line with the Stolper-Samuelson theorem. Instead, if there are limits on the extent to which real wages can fall, unemployment in the wine industry could occur sufficient to keep the real wage from declining further and consequently, the adjustment to trade would be via some unemployment and a partial decline in the real wage. Point S represents this possibility. Output of bread has expanded, that of wine has contracted. Note, however, that the new production point S lies off the efficiency locus so that production lies inside the production frontier. The corresponding production points are indicated by P', R', and S' in Figure 3–5b. The situation depicted indicates a loss in welfare relative to the self-sufficiency point as a result of trade causing unemployment. It should be noted that a protective tariff would not be an appropriate policy since consumers are taxed. Instead, a direct production subsidy to the distressed industry may be appropriate (see H. G. Johnson's [1965] article on optimal intervention in the presence of domestic distortions).

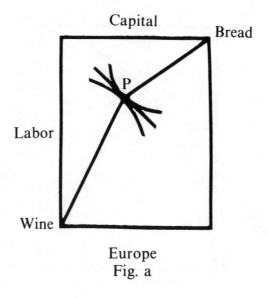

Europe
Fig. a

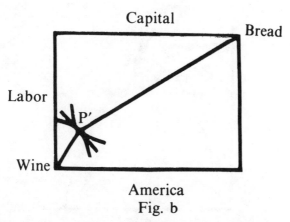

America
Fig. b

FIGURE 3-4. Factor Price Equalization. With identical production functions displaying constant returns to scale and diminishing marginal productivities, relative and absolute returns to factors of production depend solely on the factor-use ratios (with production of both commodities). Free trade equalizes relative commodity and factor prices under these conditions. At points *P* and *P'* both the relative and absolute prices of factors are equalized since the factor proportions in the two industries are identical between the two countries. Equivalently, the marginal products of labor and capital are the same at *P* and *P'*.

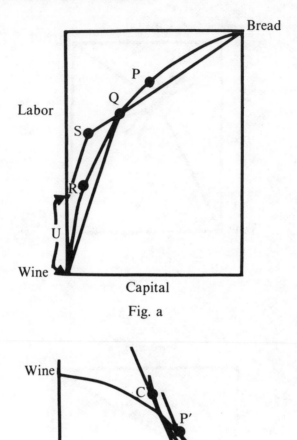

Fig. a

FIGURE 3–5. Trade and Unemployment. After real wages decline somewhat from point P to Q, they become downwardly rigid. Consequently, the importation of wine causes unemployment equal to U in the wine sector sufficient to prevent the capital-labor intensity ratios from declining further than their levels at Q, and, consequently, limiting the decline in real wages. In terms of the production and consumption possibilities, output of bread does not rise as much as with flexible real wages, but output of wine falls more. The resulting production point S′ may entail a lower welfare consumption point at C with trade as a result of unemployment.

BARRIERS TO TRADE AND FACTOR MOVEMENTS

A companion proposition to the factor price equalization theorem is that factor movements substitute perfectly for trade. Consider, for example, a situation in which trade has brought about factor price equalization. Clearly, there would be no incentive for factors to move from one country to another. Now suppose that Europe imposes a tariff on imports of bread, the capital-intensive commodity. The tariff has the initial effect of increasing the domestic price of bread in Europe and, consequently, the relative and absolute return to capital. (Take, for instance, a movement from point P' to P in Figure 3–6). Allow for capital mobility, and we would have a movement of capital from America to Europe. As a result the production frontier in Europe shifts outward in a biased manner toward greater domestic production of bread and smaller domestic production of wine at the same relative price. This follows from the Rybczynski theorem. Further, if capital is perfectly mobile, the movement will continue until factor returns are equalized. That is, European output of bread will continue to rise, and its output of wine to fall, until factor prices are once again equal. Domestic production of the import good displaces previous imports. Indeed, the displacement of imports is complete (if not, factor returns would differ because of the tariff). Production of bread will rise by an amount exactly equal to the quantity previously imported, and consumption patterns and relative prices will remain unchanged. In short, any impediment to trade will stimulate factor movements that eliminate the need for trade. The argument can be demonstrated graphically. Again, refer to Figure 3–6.

Initially, the production and consumption patterns are located at P and S, respectively. The relative price equals the slope of the line passing through the two points. The higher domestic return to capital resulting from the imposition of a tariff induces capital to move into Europe, expanding the production frontier outward along the PP' (Rybczynski) line. As long as any trade takes place, the return to capital will be higher in Europe than America, and capital movement will continue. However, when production reaches the point P', there is no longer any need for trade. The previous pattern of consumption, S, can be maintained, and the required rental payments for foreign capital, $P'S$, can be made. The value of the foreign capital in terms of wine is QR or $P'S$ at constant prices. This is so because the increase in bread production is RS, which is worth PR bottles of wine. By deducting the fall in the production of wine, PQ, from PR, we are left with QR as the marginal product of foreign capital.

In summary, any impediment to trade will bring about factor movements that eliminate the need for trade altogether. The world production and consumption patterns will be the same, and commodity and factor prices will remain unchanged. Robert Mundell (1957) has suggested this result.

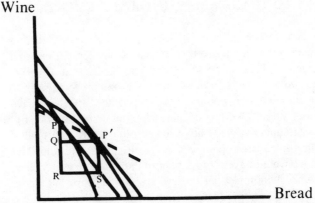

FIGURE 3–6. Barriers to Trade and Factor Mobility. Initially, production takes place at point *P* and consumption at point *S*, Europe importing *RS* loaves of bread. A tariff on bread imports has the effect of increasing the domestic relative price of bread and, at the same time, the relative and absolute return to capital. With perfect capital mobility capital flows into Europe, thereby causing the production frontier to shift outward in favor of bread, the capital-intensive commodity. The capital inflow will continue until returns are equalized at home and abroad, implying that no further movement of factors takes place once point *P'* is reached. At *P'* the value of payments for foreign capital equals *P'S* bottles of wine, so that the original consumption point *S* is maintained without any further trade being necessary. In short, barriers to trade coupled with no obstacles to factor mobility bring about factor movements that eliminate the necessity for trade altogether. Robert Mundell (1957) found this result.

FACTOR INTENSITY REVERSALS

Any account of the Heckscher-Ohlin model would be incomplete without raising the problem of reversals in factor intensities. It is entirely conceivable that a good be labor-intensive relative to another when labor is relatively cheap and capital-intensive when capital is relatively cheap. This would mean that there is greater ease of factor substitution in the production of that good. In fact, one can easily imagine two or more factor reversals in varying regions of the isoquants. The implications of the possibility of factor reversals are far-reaching.

To take a simple example, suppose that there is greater factor substitutability in the wine industry. If the factor endowment ratios are sufficiently different, wine will be labor-intensive in the labor-abundant country, and capital-intensive in the capital-abundant country. Graphically, the efficiency loci would lie on one side of the diagonal of the factor box in one country and on the other side in the second country. It would no longer be possible to identify a particular good as the capital-intensive one. Thus the Heckscher-Ohlin theorem would be difficult to interpret in a meaningful way. Furthermore, the relationship between factor and commodity prices would no longer be one to one. With sufficiently different endowment ratios, higher wine prices inducing an expansion in output in the wine industry in the labor-abundant country would cause relative and absolute wages to rise, whereas in the capital-abundant country the same expansion would cause a fall in relative and real wages. For a given commodity price ratio set by free trade, neither relative nor real returns to factors of production would be equalized. The many possibilities that arise when factor reversals are present are too numerous to discuss here. Suffice it to say that their presence invalidates the Heckscher-Ohlin theorem in its simplest form and that free trade with incomplete specialization in both countries does not lead to factor price equalization.

THE LEONTIEF PARADOX:
AN EMPIRICAL TEST OF THE HECKSCHER-OHLIN MODEL

In 1954 Wassily Leontief published an empirical test of the Heckscher-Ohlin theorem, which, to everyone's surprise, found that U.S. exports were labor-intensive relative to U.S. import-competing goods. It was thought that since the United States was clearly a capital-abundant country, the United States would therefore export capital-intensive goods. The Leontief finding contradicted the Heckscher-Ohlin theorem and has come to be known as the Leontief paradox: that is, paradoxically, the United States exports labor-intensive goods.

Table 3–1 reproduces Leontief's 1954 findings. In 1947, U.S. export industries used only $13,991 per man-year, whereas U.S. import-competing industries used $18,184 per man-year, giving a capital-labor ratio 1.3 times greater in the import-competing industry. This result was reconfirmed by Leontief and others such as Robert Baldwin (1971) in later tests of the Heckscher-Ohlin theorem, which led to great questioning as to the predictability of this model.

A number of explanations for the Leontief paradox have been offered. First,

TABLE 3–1. The Leontief Paradox:
U.S. Capital and Labor Requirements, 1947

	Capital (in dollars)	Labor (in man-years)	Capital/Labor (in dollars)
Exports	2,550,780	182.313	13,991
Imports	3,091,339	170.004	18,184

Note: Figures are given per million dollars of exports and import replacements.
Source: Adapted from Leontief 1954.

it has been suggested that U.S. labor is more efficient than foreign labor, thus offsetting Heckscher-Ohlin comparative advantage patterns. The extent to which U.S. labor would have to be more efficient than foreign labor, however—namely, more than three times—to account for this reversal does not seem plausible, neither to Leontief nor to other researchers. A second related explanation regarding the skill content of U.S. exports receives a bit more support. It is argued that U.S. labor invests heavily in human capital formation, so that U.S. exports tend to be intensive in the use of skilled labor. A third explanation seeks not to contradict the underlying supply-side argument of the Heckscher-Ohlin model but rather to argue that relatively strong preference for capital-intensive goods in U.S. consumer tastes on the demand side tends to outweigh supply-side comparative advantage. The strong preferences could be a result of higher income per capita. A fourth explanation advanced by Jaroslav Vanek (1959) is that there is a very important third factor, natural resources, that is abundant in the United States and complementary to labor as in input, leading thus to a U.S. comparative advantage in labor-intensive industries.

CONCLUSION

The Heckscher-Ohlin model is a powerful tool for analyzing the relationship between international trade and the real returns to factors of production as well as the problem of unemployment. Its main propositions are that the pattern of comparative advantage is determined by the relative abundance of factors of production and that trade will help the abundant factor, whereas it will harm the scarce factor. Under certain conditions free trade will equalize real returns to labor and capital internationally, thereby removing incentives to movements in the factors of production. On the other hand, a tariff increases the real return to the scarce factor and thus provides an incentive for an inflow of the scarce factor and an outflow of the abundant factor. In short, international trade is a substitute for factor mobility, and factor mobility is a substitute for trade.

Trade may cause unemployment of the scarce factor if its real wage is rigid downward. In some cases the extent of unemployment may be so great that it reverses the gains from trade. If so, a subsidy to the import-competing industry may be warranted.

Finally, the Leontief paradox suggests that the United States has a comparative advantage in labor-intensive goods. While this apparently contradicts the prediction of the Heckscher-Ohlin model, various factors may come into play that can offset the supply side.

SELECTED READINGS

Balassa, Bela. 1979. "The Changing Pattern of Comparative Advantage in Manufactured Goods." *Review of Economics and Statistics* (May).

Baldwin, Robert E. 1971. "Determinants of the Commodity Structure of U.S. Trade." *American Economic Review* (March).

Brecher, Richard. 1974. "Minimum Wage Rates and the Pure Theory of International Trade." *Quarterly Journal of Economics* (February).

Ethier, Wilfred. 1982. "National and International Returns to Scale and the Modern Theory of International Trade." *American Economic Review*, no. 2 (June).

Heckscher, Eli. 1919. "The Effects of Foreign Trade on the Distribution of Income." *Economisk Tidskrift*.

Johnson, Harry G. 1957. "Factor Endowments, International Trade, and Factor Prices." *Manchester School of Economic and Social Studies* (September).

———. 1965. "Optimal Intervention in the Presence of Domestic Distortions." In *Trade, Growth and the Balance of Payments: Essays in Honor of Gottfried Haberler*, edited by Robert Baldwin, et. al. Chicago: Rand McNally.

Jones, Ronald. 1956/57. "Factor Proportions and the Heckscher-Ohlin Theorem." *Review of Economic Studies*.

Kenen, Peter. 1965. "Nature, Capital, and Trade." *Journal of Political Economy* (October).

Lancaster, Kelvin. 1957. "The Heckscher-Ohlin Trade Model: A Geometric Treatment." *Economica* (February).

Leamer, E. E. 1980. "The Leontief Paradox Reconsidered." *Journal of Political Economy*, no. 3.

Leontief, Wassily. 1954. "Domestic Production and Foreign Trade: The American Capital Position Re-Examined." *Economia Internazionale* 7.

Mundell, Robert. 1957. "International Trade and Factor Mobility." *American Economic Review* (June).

Ohlin, Bertil. 1933. *Interregional and International Trade*. Cambridge, Mass.: Harvard University Press.

Robinson, Romney. 1956. "Factor Proportions and Comparative Advantage." *Quarterly Journal of Economics* (May).

Rybczynski, T. M. 1955. "Factor Endowments and Relative Commodity Prices." *Economica* (November).

Samuelson, Paul. 1949. "International Factor Price Equalization Once Again." *Economic Journal* (June).

Savosnik, Kurt. 1958. "The Box Diagram and the Production Possibility Curve." *Economisk Tidskrift*.

Stern, Robert. 1975. "Testing Trade Theories." In *International Trade and Finance*, edited by Peter Kenen. Cambridge: At the University Press.

Stolper, Wolfgang, and Paul Samuelson. 1941. "Protection and Real Wages." *Review of Economic Studies* (November).

Vanek, Jaroslav. 1959. "The National Resource Content of Foreign Trade, 1870-1955, and the Relative Abundance of Natural Resources in the United States." *Review of Economics and Statistics*, no. 2.

Williams, J. R. 1970. "The Resource Content in International Trade." *Canadian Economic Journal*, no. 2.

FOUR

INTERNATIONAL TRADE AND THE EFFICIENCY CONDITIONS

When it is not possible to improve the welfare of one person or country without lowering the welfare of another, a situation is said to be *Pareto optimal*. This chapter adopts the Pareto criterion of economic efficiency and applies it to international trade. Specifically, it is shown that with increasing opportunity costs and no externalities, a situation of free trade is Pareto optimal from a worldwide point of view. Trade equalizes opportunity costs of production worldwide, thereby satisfying the conditions of production efficiency, and faces all consumers with the same set of relative prices, thereby satisfying the conditions of consumption optimality. In this context a case can be made for free trade. In what follows we develop the conditions for production and consumption efficiency and deal with special cases that pose problems such as decreasing opportunity costs.

PRODUCTION EFFICIENCY: INCREASING OPPORTUNITY COSTS

The notion of efficiency and optimality are sometimes quite difficult to pin down. To avoid ambiguity, let us think first of all of *production efficiency* as a situation in which the maximum obtainable amount of one good is reached, for any given levels of output of other goods and employment of inputs. By definition, it is a purely technological relationship describing the most possible that can be obtained from a given hypothetical situation and is frequently summarized by the familiar production possibility frontier. Figure 4–1 depicts a case of increasing opportunity costs of production.

A production frontier is drawn for a given state of technology, a given employment of resources, and serves as a hypothetical benchmark by which to judge the performance of an economic system. As such, it is hard to divorce the con-

Bread

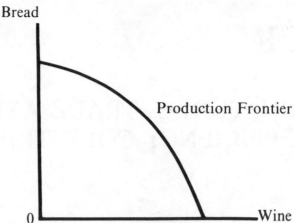

Production Frontier

0   Wine

FIGURE 4-1. Increasing Opportunity Costs. The production frontier is bowed toward the origin, or concave, displaying increasing opportunity costs of production. This means that an efficient shuffling of resources from the bread to the wine industry causes ever greater sacrifices in terms of bread. In the Ricardian model, increasing opportunity costs could arise if there were diminishing average productivities of labor. In the Heckscher-Ohlin model with constant returns to scale in both industries, opportunity costs increase because the price of the factor intensive to a particular industry increases as that industry expands.

cept from one of bestness since we are accustomed to think that more is better than less.

A production frontier has one other property that we might bring up now. It can never have a positive slope. This would mean that more of both goods could be had. If this were true, we would not be on the frontier. It is just a matter of definition. Suppose, for example, we increase bread production by one loaf by reshuffling resources and, in doing so, get an extra bottle of wine. By throwing away the loaf, we have the same amount of bread as before and, in addition, an extra bottle of wine. We could not, therefore, have had the maximum amount of wine in the first place. It follows that we were not on the frontier. By the same token the production frontier cannot be flat. In short, it must have a negative slope, indicating that efficiency implies that more of one good entails a sacrifice of the other.

The *transformation function,* as it is also known, can assume, in principle, any curvature or combination of curvatures consistent with a negative slope. In practice, it is usually assumed to bow away from the origin—or to be concave. This reflects the assumption that if more and more wine is to be produced, even greater sacrifices of bread must be made. Implicit in this is the notion that the more resources committed to one pursuit, the less adaptable are the remaining resources. This is variously called the *law of diminishing marginal rate of trans-*

formation or *increasing opportunity cost,* which simply means that the slope or opportunity cost of wine in terms of bread is increasingly steep, moving left to right. But, we must be careful in interpreting the slope of the production frontier. It indicates the maximum amount of additional wine obtainable by a small additional sacrifice of bread. In other words it implies an efficient reshuffling of resources, and it is not just the commonplace observation that things are increasingly costly. It means that, but it also means that they are increasingly costly even when efficiently acquired.

We could go behind our transformation schedules and look more closely into what conditions must be satisfied to reach them. Assuming that the best technology available is used, and that all resources are fully employed, efficiency requires equal marginal rates of substitution between factors of production in both industries. In what follows we assume that the economy operates at a point on its production frontier.

Assuming we have both production frontiers, we seek to describe the characteristics of efficient production patterns. The answer follows from comparative advantage. If both countries produce both goods—for example, are not completely specialized—the opportunity cost of production must be the same. This is so for a very simple reason: If the opportunity costs were different, the output of all goods could be increased. Suppose, for example, that in America the opportunity (or marginal) cost of a bottle of wine is two loaves of bread, whereas it is one and one-half in Europe. By expanding wine production one bottle in Europe and contracting production one bottle in America, a net gain of one-half loaf of bread is realized. This is, in fact, Ricardo's celebrated principle of comparative advantage in another guise. If in the absence of trade the pattern of opportunity costs were as indicated above, Europe has a comparative advantage in wine, and America in bread. By specializing accordingly, they stand to gain since more of both wine and bread can be produced. In the Ricardian case, however, the elimination of the comparative advantage through trade typically brings about complete specialization, at least for one country, because the opportunity costs are assumed to be constant. That is, the production frontiers are straight lines.

In the case of increasing opportunity costs, the elimination of comparative advantage (or the equality of opportunity costs) need not entail complete specialization. As wine production is expanded in Europe and contracted in America, opportunity costs measured in bread rise in the former and fall in the latter. They may therefore be brought into equality before complete specialization results. Indeed, this equality is the efficiency criterion. As long as it is not satisfied, more of both goods can be obtained. We have, then, the rule that if both countries produce both goods, efficiency requires equality of opportunity costs of production. This rule gives us a way to find a world production frontier indicating in exactly the same way as the national frontier the most of one good that can be obtained for a given amount of the other. Figure 4–2 illustrates the rule of production efficiency.

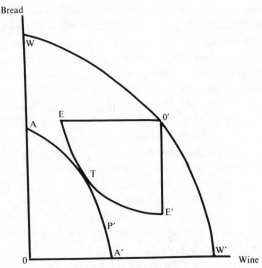

FIGURE 4–2. Production Efficiency. If two countries produce two goods, production efficiency requires that the opportunity costs of production be equal, as at the point of tangency, T, of America's production frontier and Europe's inverted production frontier. Thus by sliding Europe's frontier along America's, the world possibility frontier, WW', is derived. Beyond a certain point, it is efficient for one of the countries to cease production of a particular good. From A' to P', Europe completely specializes in wine production, whereas America produces both wine and bread. The first loaves of bread are produced by America beginning at A' until the opportunity cost of producing bread in America rises at P' to equal the opportunity cost of Europe producing its first loaves of bread. Similarly, in the northwest portion of the world production frontier, America initially specializes in bread production.

Since the slope of a transformation curve represents opportunity costs of production, efficiency requires equality of slopes. This is reflected in the tangency of America's production frontier with Europe's inverted frontier. The origin of the latter represents, then, one point on the world possibility frontier. This point is found by adding up the production of each good in each country. Sliding Europe's frontier along America's locus of points traced out by Europe's origin, O', will indicate the world frontier. The world frontier, in turn, has properties similar to the underlying national ones. It has, for example, the same slope as AA' and EE' in the region of incomplete specialization.

In other words, if both countries produce both goods, extra amounts of any good can be had at the same cost in both countries. However, that is not the entire story. After some point efficiency may require complete specialization by at least one country. Indeed, so long as the production curves are not identical, there must be regions of complete specialization on the world frontier. This is so because as world production of, say, wine increases, the costs of providing any bread at all by the country relatively more efficient in wine production will eventually exceed the opportunity costs of bread produced abroad. It must then cease to produce bread completely. Graphically, this means that the production frontiers, while no longer tangent, are still in contact. Such a region is traced out by O' from the corresponding point of contact P' downward to A' where both countries produce only wine. Moving northwest from A', America produces the first loaves of bread, whereas Europe continues to specialize in wine production. This is so because the opportunity cost of producing extra loaves of bread in America is lower than in Europe in this region. Eventually, at P' the opportunity cost of producing extra bread in America rises to equal the opportunity cost of the first loaves in Europe, so bread production in Europe begins. Similarly, in the northwest portion of the world production frontier, America initially specializes in bread production.

DECREASING OPPORTUNITY COSTS

Before moving on to the problem of consumption efficiency, we should first deal with the problem of decreasing opportunity costs—a transformation curve that is bowed or convex to the origin. Now this is not necessarily an insurmountable problem if everybody knows that this is so. That is, if they know the exact configuration of the frontier. It becomes one, however, in the presence of atomistic competition and imperfect knowledge. Firms faced with given market prices will tend to specialize in one good. This may not be efficient for two reasons: complete specialization may not be warranted; and even if it is, it might be better to specialize in another direction. Unwarranted specialization may occur because, with given prices, a position of incomplete specialization represents profit minimization to the firm and is thus not a position attainable by market forces. Specialization in the wrong direction can occur because both end points may satisfy local conditions of profit maximization, thus being attainable positions, whereas one has a higher global profit than the other. These possibilities are shown in Figure 4–3.

The production frontier is everywhere convex to the origin, implying that any point of incomplete specialization is not attainable by atomistic competition. Complete specialization, however, may be in either direction. Take, for instance, the relative price indicated by the two parallel lines drawn from the end points of the production frontier. Complete specialization in wine is a sustainable market outcome since any small movement in the production of any bread at all causes losses to be incurred. Similarly, complete specialization in bread is an attainable possibility since movements in the direction of wine production cause losses. From a global point of view, however, with the relative price taken as given,

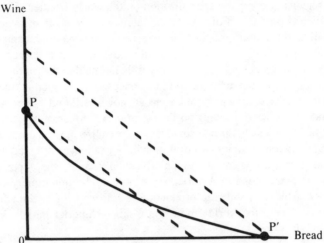

FIGURE 4-3. Decreasing Opportunity Costs. As drawn, the production frontier displays decreasing opportunity costs everywhere. As more and more bread is produced, less and less wine has to be sacrificed. Faced with a world price such as that indicated by the parallel broken lines, the country would specialize in production. However, it may specialize in wine production rather than in bread production, thereby having a lower value of national income than if it specialized in the opposite direction. This results since both points of complete specialization represent local profit maximization, whereas global profit maximization would require specialization in, and the export of, bread.

for example, by the world market, the value of national income is higher with complete specialization in the production of bread. Thus, in a trade setting the country should specialize in bread and import wine for domestic consumption, but it may specialize in wine and import bread.

A country need not always specialize in the presence of decreasing opportunity costs. In particular a production frontier may have regions in which opportunity costs of production are alternatively increasing, then decreasing, in innumerable combinations. To illustrate the importance of such cases, consider the curvature of the production frontier in Figure 4-4.

Initially, the production of bread takes place subject to increasing costs, but beyond a certain level of production decreasing costs prevail. If producers in America behave competitively but do not have perfect knowledge on the curvature of the production frontier, a production point such as P is attainable with a world price equal to the slope of the parallel lines. This is so since the point P is one of local profit maximization. Consumption may take place at point Q through trade at the world price ratio—America thereby importing bread in ex-

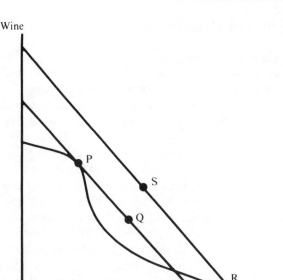

FIGURE 4–4. Varying Costs of Production. Initially, the production frontier is concave, implying increasing opportunity costs of bread production. If sufficient quantities of bread are produced, however, the frontier becomes convex and decreasing opportunity costs prevail. Faced with a world price equal to the slope of the parallel lines, a production point *P* and a consumption point *Q* are attainable with competition in the absence of perfect information. However, production at *R* and consumption at *S* is potentially superior. At the world price America should optimally specialize in and export bread, thereby realizing the savings resulting from decreasing opportunity costs.

change for exports of wine. However, faced by the same world price, America should specialize in the production of bread at *R* and export bread instead of wine, thereby reaching a potentially superior consumption point *S*. A point of incomplete specialization such as at *P* is an inferior one because by expanding bread production America can realize gains as a result of decreasing costs. In short, rather than producing and exporting wine, America should produce and export only bread. Furthermore, even if the direction of comparative advantage were not the wrong one—that is, America produces at *P* but exports bread—the same gains are to be had by moving toward the production of only bread and increasing the volume of trade in wine. Finally, we should note that a large number of possible local optima may arise with varying curvature of the production frontier. With a given world price there will, except by accident, be only one pattern of production that maximizes the value of the country's production. Furthermore, this point need not involve complete specialization in production.

CONSUMPTION OPTIMALITY

We are now ready to sketch the conditions necessary for efficient consumption of goods, bearing in mind that there is no unique best level of consumption. This is so because Pareto optimality is our benchmark—that is, situations in which the well-being of one individual cannot be increased without harming someone else. To put the matter in a different way, it is much the same sort of thing that arises in defining the *production frontier*. The production frontier indicates a set of efficient production possibilities without singling out any particular pattern of production as the favored one. In this light we can think of *consumption efficiency* as finding the situation most preferred by one individual for any arbitrarily chosen set of situations among which other individuals are indifferent. If we make use of our handy index, the utility function, this involves finding the maximum level of utility possible for one individual corresponding to each level of utility registered by other individuals. But this maximization process must take place within the realm of the possible: goods are not available in unlimited quantities. And, these possibilities are set forth in the production frontier, so that, in short, we must take into account this production constraint.

In what follows we treat countries as though they were individuals. In other words we will use utility indexes for the purpose of describing the preferences of a nation. The problem of optimality in consumption involves, then, finding the maximum utility of one country for each level of utility enjoyed by the other. Suppose we arbitrarily select a set of consumption possibilities such as along I_A in Figure 4–5 among which America is indifferent. That is, along this curve America's utility index registers the same amount of satisfaction. The particular amount registered is chosen completely arbitrarily. This curve of indifference traces out combinations of bread and wine that are equally desirable to America and is drawn so that it is convex to the origin, reflecting the assumption that as more and more of one good is sacrificed, larger and larger amounts of the other must be consumed to compensate exactly for additional sacrifices. This assumption is known as the *law of the diminishing marginal rate of substitution*.

We also assume that the total quantities of bread and wine must be divided up between the two countries. If we phrase this in terms of trade theory, exports of either good entail a corresponding sacrifice in domestic consumption. We have already set down the production efficiency conditions: they are incorporated in the world production frontier WW' transferred to Figure 4–5.

We must now add to this building block, in step-by-step fashion, the conditions of consumption efficiency. First, notice that the world production pattern indicated by point Q and the origin O form diagonally opposed corners of a rectangle whose sides represent the volume of output of each good. The question we seek to answer is, For this production pattern, what is the greatest possible satisfaction in Europe for the level of satisfaction corresponding to I_A in

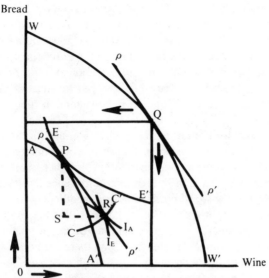

FIGURE 4–5. **Production and Consumption Efficiency.** As a necessary condition for efficiency, the opportunity costs of production must be everywhere equal if both countries produce both goods. As before, this is embodied in the tangency at point *P* of the production frontiers. Consumption efficiency requires that the marginal social rates of indifference in both countries be equal: that is, that both goods have the same value in consumption in each country. Production and consumption efficiency taken together require, in addition, that the opportunity costs in production equal the marginal rates of indifference in consumption, as indicated by the slope of the line ρρ drawn through *P* and *R*. The diagram can also serve to depict the free trade setting. The terms of trade are ρρ′, the production point is *P*, and the consumption pattern is *R*. Consequently, America exports *PS* loaves of bread to Europe in exchange for *SR* bottles of wine. Trade balances at the price ratio ρρ′ since the supplies and demands for imports just coincide. Thus, in this setting free trade satisfies the production and consumption efficiency conditions.

America? First let us see how we can find an easy answer from our production box. If the sides represent world outputs, then they must be divided up between American and European consumption. To make this division clear, let *O* represent America's consumption origin, so that the arrows represent directions of increasing consumption by America, and let *Q* serve as the origin of Europe's (inverted) consumption pattern, the arrows indicating increasing consumption in Europe. This gives us the famous Edgeworth-Bowley box diagram used to describe the conditions of pure exchange. Any point inside the box represents a division of world outputs. But we are only interested in those along *I_A* for the moment. America is indifferent to any division traced out by this curve. However, which of these is most preferable to Europe? This point is indicated by the highest (inverted) indifference curve of Europe, I_E, touching America's indifference curve at R. It represents the best situation for Europe, corresponding to the arbitrarily chosen level of welfare in America implicit in I_A. At point R the two indifference curves are tangent; that is, their slopes are equal. This implies equality of the marginal rates of substitution in consumption, for that is how these rates are defined.

Had we chosen a different initial level of welfare for America, the same criterion would apply, but the point described would involve a different, but nonetheless efficient, consumption distribution. In other words it is possible to trace out a locus of points along which the indifference curves are tangent and equal to the slope of the world production frontier, thereby forming a consumption efficiency curve. This curve, CC', is often called the *contract curve of efficient exchanges*. Along CC' all marginal rates of transformation in production and substitution in consumption are equal, and there are no possible alternative exchanges that are mutually advantageous to both countries. Any point off the curve, on the other hand, is not an optimal one. This is easily seen because two indifference curves would intersect rather than be tangent, their arcs thereby carving out a core inside of which there are points preferable to both. In short, any situation involving inequality of the marginal rates of substitution in consumption can potentially be improved upon. Like the production efficiency rule, this criterion holds only for cases where both goods are consumed in those countries.

It is entirely possible that a situation might arise where it would be efficient for one or both of the countries to consume only one of the goods, and this is possible even if both indifference curves are convex. Part of the CC' curve would lie on one of the edges of the box. In such cases the consumption efficiency criterion becomes one of inequality. For the production pattern Q, consumption efficiency requires equality of the marginal rates of substitution in consumption if both goods are consumed everywhere and inequality if specialization in consumption takes place. Conceptually, it is the same thing as in production, so we will not go further into the problem.

PRODUCTION AND CONSUMPTION EFFICIENCY

This, then, is the consumption efficiency rule to be added to the production efficiency rule derived in the last section. It would appear that our job of deriving the general Pareto efficiency conditions is finished. But it is not: one last step is necessary. It involves, for the case of production and consumption of both goods everywhere, bringing into equality the marginal rates of transformation in production and consumption, or

$$MRS^A_{xy} = MRS^E_{xy} = MC^A_{xy} = MC^E_{xy}.$$

Specifically, not only must the respective opportunity costs of production be equal, and the corresponding rates of substitution in consumption be equal, but they must also equal each other. For if the rates of production sacrifice and consumption sacrifice were not equal, this would mean that output of the goods could be increased at a smaller sacrifice in terms of the other than that necessary to keep both countries as well off as before. To put the matter differently, both countries could be more than compensated for an increase in the production of the good whose opportunity cost is less than its marginal rate of consumption indifference.

Graphically, this means that the consumption point must lie on the contract curve and that the production point must lie on the production frontier but that these points must also correspond to each other in a particular way: the lines of tangency running through them must be parallel. In Figure 4–5 a particular case of this is drawn where the line tangent to the two production blocks is also tangent to the two indifference curves. This ensures equality of opportunity costs in production and consumption.

It is, in fact, the picture trade theorists have in mind in arguing for free trade as the optimal situation for the world as a whole. Free trade brings into equality relative prices, or rates of exchange, in production, consumption, and exchange, all represented by the slope of the line $\varrho\varrho'$, thereby satisfying the world Pareto efficiency conditions. In this situation it is not possible to make one country better off at no expense to others in abandoning free trade. It is in this sense, efficiency for the world taken as a whole, that the free trade argument is made. Production patterns are represented by point P, and consumption patterns by R. Imports are the difference between consumption and production at home, so that America imports wine in exchange for exports of bread. Trade is in balance since desired exports of one equal desired exports of the other at the terms of trade $\varrho\varrho'$.

CONCLUSION

We have developed the conditions of production and consumption efficiency in an international setting. When countries produce the same good, production efficiency requires that their marginal rates of substitution between that good and other goods be the same. With increasing opportunity costs and no externalities free trade satisfies the conditions of production and consumption efficiency— and thus is superior to a tariff-ridden situation since it is not possible to make anyone better off without injuring someone else. In short, free trade is Pareto optimal under these circumstances.

With decreasing opportunity costs a country may specialize in the wrong direction, thereby not fully benefitting from international trade and specialization according to the principle of comparative advantage.

SELECTED READINGS

Basevi, Giorgio. 1970. "Domestic Demand and Ability to Export." *Journal of Political Economy* (March-April).

Ethier, Wilfred. 1982. "National and International Returns to Scale and the Modern Theory of International Trade." *American Economic Review* (June).

Kemp, Murray. 1969. *The Pure Theory of International Trade and Investment.* Englewood Cliffs, N.J.: Prentice-Hall, chap. 8.

Lerner, Abba. 1932. "The Diagrammatical Representation of Cost Conditions in International Trade." *Economica* (August).

Matthews, R. C. O. 1949/50. "Reciprocal Demand and Increasing Returns." *Review of Economic Studies.*

Meade, James. 1952. *A Geometry of International Trade.* London: George Allen and Unwin.

FIVE

TRADE EQUILIBRIUM

In the previous chapter we left off with a short sketch of trade equilibrium and its welfare characteristics. To make the picture complete, this chapter treats some aspects of trade equilibrium in greater depth and puts the trade apparatus to work on problems of tariffs, quotas, and foreign retaliation. The first section develops the famous Marshallian offer curve and discusses its properties. The elasticity of the offer curve is derived, and trade equilibrium is shown by the use of offer curves for America and Europe. The stability of the equilibrium is examined, giving the famous Marshall-Lerner condition that the sum of the import elasticities of demand must be greater than one for stability. The second part applies the offer curve analysis to commercial policy, putting the accent on the impact of tariffs and quotas upon the international terms of trade and the domestic relative price ratio. The third part introduces a nontraded goods sector, which highlights the importance of the price of home versus international goods in the process of adjustment following shocks such as money supply increases and devaluations. The nontraded goods model is also used to illustrate the absorption approach to the balance of payments and is applied to the debt problem in this context.

THE OFFER CURVE

An *offer curve* is simply a supply curve of exports: it depicts the quantity of exports supplied at various relative prices. It differs from a typical supply curve only in the way it is depicted geometrically: the quantity of imports demanded is represented on the opposite axis rather than their price. Otherwise, there is no substantial difference between an offer curve and a demand (or supply) curve. If an individual demands one thing—for example, bread—this person must at the same time supply another—for instance, money—in exchange. Or, the trade could be of a pure barter nature: the individual simultaneously supplies wine and demands bread. The price, or terms of trade, is simply the number of loaves of bread the individual receives in return for each bottle of wine he or she gives up. The same information can be obtained from the usual demand curve drawn as a function of the relative price of a good. The supply of the other good, be it money or wine, is the product of the price and the quantity of bread demanded. Consequently, if the demand curve for bread is elastic, the supply curve for wine has a positive slope. If the demand curve has a unitary elasticity, price times quantity demanded is a constant, and the supply of wine is constant. Finally, if the demand for bread is inelastic, the supply curve of wine is negatively sloped. The purpose of an offer curve is to depict this relationship graphically by simultaneously indicating the supply of exports and the demand for imports. Examine Figure 5–1.

In Figure 5–1a America's production possibility frontier AA' is drawn, along with the autarkic production and consumption point P,C. The pretrade relative price is indicated by the slope of the line passing through P,C. Consider the experiment of facing America with a slightly lower foreign price of wine, such as that indicated by the less steep slope of $P'C'$. At a lower relative price of wine, America has a comparative advantage in bread, the production point moves to P' with bread production expanding and wine production contracting. Notice in passing that complete specialization need not take place with increasing opportunity costs. The consumption point moves to C', $O'C'$ bottles of wine imports are demanded in exchange for $O'P'$ loaves of bread exports at the foreign relative price $P'C'$.

The trade triangle $P'O'C'$ illustrates the supply of bread exports and, at the same time, the demand for wine imports. Transfer this triangle to Figure 5–1b, bread exports equaling $O'P'$ along the vertical axis and wine imports equaling $C'O'$ along the horizontal axis. The terms of trade, the number of loaves of bread exported per bottle of wine imported, equals the slope of $C'P'$, that is, $O'P'/C'O'$ in Figure b. We can duplicate the same experiment by letting America engage in trade at even more favorable terms; through the slope of $P''C''$ in Figure 5–1a construct the trade triangle $P''O''C''$, then invert and transfer it to Figure 5–1b to get America's new offer of exports of bread and demand for imports of wine at the price $O''P''/C''O''$.

By considering all possible price ratios—that is, rotating the price lines in figures 5–1a and 5–1b—and tracing out the locus of the trading points C', C'', and so forth, we get America's offer curve of bread exports, the curve OF of wine in Figure 5–b. America would have had a comparative advantage in wine and a corresponding offer curve that would simultaneously indicate its supply of exports and demand for imports as a function of the world price.

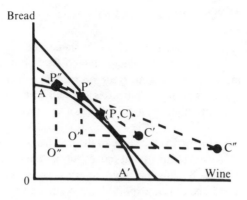

Fig. a

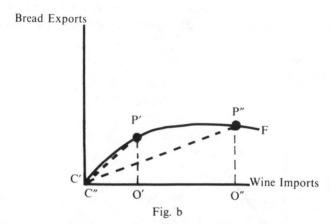

Fig. b

FIGURE 5–1.   Derivation of an Offer Curve. In the absence of trade the
production and consumption patterns must be identical, such as at the point P,C.
The line tangent to this point is the price ratio that reigns with self-sufficiency.
At a lower price of wine, such as depicted by the less steep slope of the line
$P'C'$, the production point moves toward greater production of bread at P' and,
as drawn, to greater consumption of wine at C'. At the new price ratio, therefore, desired bread exports are $O'P'$, and desired wine imports are $O'C'$. The
axes of this trade triangle can be transferred to Figure 5–1*b* where the supply
of bread exports is indicated along the vertical axis, and the demand for wine
imports is given along the horizontal axis. A second trade triangle can be derived by facing the economy with an even lower price of wine $P''C''$ and transferred in the same fashion, thereby giving a second point on the country's offer
curve. By considering all such price ratios, and joining the desired trading points,
the offer curve of the economy is laid out in Figure 5–1*b*.

PROPERTIES OF AN OFFER CURVE

An offer curve can assume many different shapes and curvatures. Some of the more unusual patterns arise from decreasing costs of production; others from the impact of changes in the terms of trade on income distribution and, consequently, demand patterns. For our purposes we will take a relatively well behaved offer curve having both positive and negative sloped regions, as shown in Figure 5–2.

The price of wine imports is the slope of the line from the origin to any trading point such as *P*. As the trading point moves further out along the offer curve, the terms of trade of the bread-exporting country become progressively better: fewer loaves of bread need to be exported per bottle of wine imported. In the positively sloped region emanating from the trade origin *O*, the supply of bread exports rises with an increase in their price. At the maximum point, *M*, a small change in the terms of trade causes no change in the quantity of bread exports supplied; and in the negatively sloped region to the right of *M*, an increased price

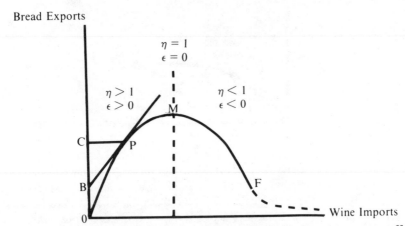

FIGURE 5–2. Properties of an Offer Curve. Initially, the country offers more bread for more wine up to a maximum point *M*, at which less bread is offered for increasing wine imports. The elasticity of demand for wine imports, η, is OC/OB, and the elasticity of supply of bread exports, ϵ, is BC/OB, at the trading point *P*. Further, since $OC/OB - BC/OB = OB/OB$, or unity, the elasticity of demand for exports minus the elasticity of supply of exports equals 1, or $\eta - \epsilon = 1$. Notice two other relationships: (1) as long as there is some price high enough to choke off all demand for imports, the offer curve must pass through the origin; and (2) as long as demand is insatiable, the offer curve cannot intersect the horizontal axis elsewhere. The latter relationship is depicted by the broken-line portion of the offer curve.

of bread causes reduced export supplies. In terms of elasticities the supply of exports is initially price elastic, then has a zero elasticity, and finally has a negative elasticity. In terms of the demand for wine imports, expenditures of bread initially rise, are constant, then fall with lower prices of wine imports. So we may say that the demand is initially elastic or exceeds 1, equals unity at point M, and then becomes inelastic. The regions are indicated likewise in the graph.

Draw a line BP tangent to the point P on the offer curve. At the point P the elasticity of demand for wine imports equals the ratio OC/OB, and that of the elasticity of supply of bread exports equals BC/OB. In the positively sloped region, $OC/OB > 1$, so the elasticity of demand would exceed unity and the elasticity of supply would be positive; at the maximum point the demand elasticity would equal 1 since $OC/OB = 1$ at M, and the supply elasticity zero; and past M the elasticity of demand would be < 1 and the supply elasticity negative (note that BC is negative in the third case). Furthermore, if we deduct the supply elasticity from the demand elasticity as defined in this way, then

$$\eta - \epsilon = \frac{OC}{OB} - \frac{BC}{OB} = \frac{OB}{OB} = 1,$$

or the elasticity of import demand exceeds the elasticity of export supply by unity. We will thus take these geometric relationships as being correct, without having proven them in detail. (James Meade [1952] has a rigorous proof.)

We might make two last remarks. First, as long as demand is insatiable, the offer curve extended cannot touch the import axis. This is so since the price of wine imports approaches zero as the terms of trade are rotated toward the wine import axis, and with insatiable demand the demand for imports must approach an infinite amount. The broken-line extension of the offer curve depicts this. Second, the offer curve must start at the origin, provided that there is some price of imports that will be high enough to choke off all demand for imports of wine in America. That price is indicated by the slope of the offer curve at the trade origin O. We will make both of these assumptions without exploring them at length.

TRADE EQUILIBRIUM AND STABILITY

We are now in a position to depict trade equilibrium with the use of Marshallian offer curves. We need only add Europe's offer curve of wine for bread to the picture, OE, and find those terms of trade that satisfy the demand and supply for imports in both countries. This is shown in Figure 5-3, where the amounts of the goods traded are indicated along the axes. At point P the number of bottles of wine that Europeans wish to export equals the number of bottles that Americans desire to import at the equilibrium terms of trade, the slope

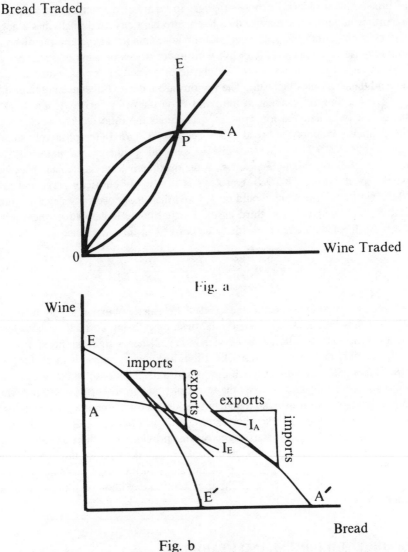

Fig. a

Fig. b

FIGURE 5-3. Trade Equilibrium. Figure 5-3a illustrates a simple case of trade equilibrium. America's offer curve of bread for wine, *OA*, intersects Europe's offer curve of wine for bread, *OE*, at point *P*. At this intersection the supplies and demands for imports are just equal, so that *P* is a point of trade balance and the equilibrium terms of trade equal the slope of the line *OP*. Figure 5-3b illustrates the corresponding production and consumption points. The trade triangles are equal at the international terms of trade (note that *a* and *b* are drawn on a slightly different scale).

of OP. At the intersection of the offer curves, the trade triangles are identical, and there is no tendency for the terms of trade to move in either direction.

An interesting question now arises: What if the relative price of the goods does not conform to the equilibrium one? Are there not forces tending to push the terms of trade back into line with those at equilibrium? The answer to this question is not so simple because the possibilities are numerous. Before getting into them, however, we have to have some sort of dynamic behavioral rule that tells us what happens when the price called out is not an equilibrium one. Let us take as a rule that when the desired export supply of wine falls short of the import demand, the price of wine rises. The situation is equivalent to an excess supply of bread on the world market since we are dealing with only two goods. In Figure 5-4a we take up the simplest case. At the terms of trade OP, American demand for wine exceeds European supply (or, equivalently, American bread supply exceeds European demand). The excess demand for wine pushes up its price, which in turn reduces the excess demand for wine. The price continues to rise until the intersection of the offer curves is reached, at which point the disequilibrium is eliminated and no forces push the price away from its position of rest. Similarly, any excess supply of wine would be eliminated by a fall in its price, so that Figure 5-4a depicts a situation of a single, stable trade equilibrium. The arrows in the diagram serve to indicate the direction of the force exerted on price by the equilibrium.

Figure 5-4b illustrates an unusual case of equilibrium. The offer curves coincide with one another over a range of prices rather than intersecting at a single one. In this range the trade patterns are in equilibrium since no excess demand or supply exists. Consequently, any price in the range is an equilibrium one, and there are no forces tending to cause it to change. If, by chance, a different price came about that was still in the range of coincidence of the offer curves, this new price would be an equilibrium one. This type of stability is termed *meta-stability*. If, for instance, one pushed a piece of chalk along a flat surface, it would eventually come to a new stable resting position. It is an easy exercise to verify that in this borderline case the sum of the elasticities of import demand equals unity, or $\eta_a + \eta_e = 1$. Thus, for stability the sum of the import elasticities of demand must exceed unity. By proving that the sum of the elasticities of import demand equal unity in the borderline or meta-stable case, we can verify that an equilibrium is stable or unstable, depending upon whether or not the sum of $\eta_a + \eta_e$ is greater than or less than unity. See Figure 5-5.

Figure 5-4c illustrates a case in which the sum of the elasticities of demand fall short of 1 at point Q. A slightly lower price of wine than that implied by the trading point induces an excess supply of wine, thereby driving its price downward. Can the fall in the price of wine induce ever greater excess supplies, thereby driving its price to zero? Clearly not, if we maintain our two previous assumptions: the demand for wine is insatiable in America (A's offer curve eventually curves upward to the left), and there is some price of wine so low that

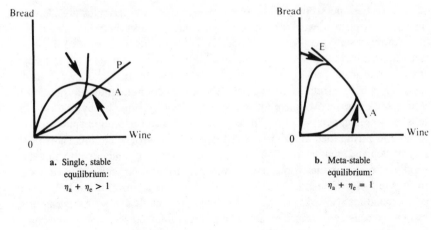

a. Single, stable
equilibrium:
$\eta_a + \eta_e > 1$

b. Meta-stable
equilibrium:
$\eta_a + \eta_e = 1$

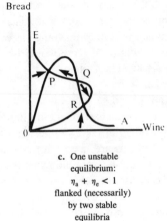

c. One unstable
equilibrium:
$\eta_a + \eta_e < 1$
flanked (necessarily)
by two stable
equilibria

FIGURE 5-4. Trade Stability. Adopting the dynamic rule that the price of a good rises when there is an excess of demand over supply, we can broadly characterize three types of equilibria. Figure 5-4a illustrates a case of a single, stable equilibrium. An excess demand for wine (or excess supply of bread) at the price *OP* is eliminated by a rise in the relative price of wine. Equilibrium is restored at the point of intersection of the offer curves. Figure 5-4b depicts a case of meta-stable equilibrium where the offer curves of America and Europe coincide along a certain range, thereby allowing for a multiplicity of equilibrium prices. Finally, Figure 5-4c has an unstable equilibrium point *Q* at which any excess demand causes a fall in price rather than a rise. However, if we suppose that demand is always insatiable, and there is always some price of imports high enough to choke off all import demand, there must exist two stable equilibria, at points *P* and *R*, flanking the unstable equilibrium. In all instances the dynamic forces on price are indicated by the direction in which the arrows point.

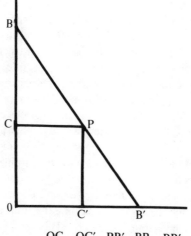

$$\eta_a + \eta_e = \frac{OC}{OB} + \frac{OC'}{OB'} = \frac{PB'}{BB'} + \frac{BP}{BB'} = \frac{BB'}{BB'} = 1$$

FIGURE 5–5.   The Marshall-Lerner Stability Condition. For the borderline case of stability, we have $\eta_a + \eta_e = OC/OB + OC'/OB' = PB'/BB' + BP/BB' = BB'/BB' = 1$. In short, for the meta-stable case, the sum of the elasticities of demand equals 1. Consequently, stability requires $\eta_a + \eta_e > 1$, which is known as the Marshall-Lerner stability condition.

Europe will supply none at all (that price indicated by the slope of E's offer curve at the origin). Taken together, these two assumptions guarantee that the offer curves must intersect at some lower price of wine such as that entailed by the point R. Further, any price lower than that will cause an excess demand for wine, thereby restoring equilibrium at point R. By an identical argument, there must exist some stable trading pattern P that flanks the unstable equilibrium Q on the other side. This has been shown by Bhagwati and Johnson (1960). The arrows summarize the forces on price in the third case of multiple equilibrium.

To summarize, then, a trade equilibrium is stable if the sum of the elasticities of import demand exceed 1, whereas it is unstable if the sum is less than 1. However, if the equilibrium is unstable, it must be flanked by stable equilibria. For the remainder of our discussion, we will take it for granted that the equilibrium position is a stable one.

TARIFFS AND QUOTAS

We have now set up the trade apparatus, and we are in a position to bring it to bear on the problems of commercial policy: tariffs and quotas. We will first concentrate on the positive aspects of commercial policy, then turn to its welfare implications in chapter 6. Until now we have assumed free trade in the absence of all impediments such as transport costs, tariffs, quotas, and the like. Starting from this position, what would be the impact on trade patterns and domestic and world prices if America imposed, for instance, an ad valorem tariff on imports of wine from Europe? That is, America collects some percentage of the price of each bottle of wine imported. If the price of wine remained unchanged, its domestic price would have to rise in a percentage amount equal to the tariff, and presumably this would cause repercussions on production and consumption decisions in America. But there are two other aspects of the problem that we have to worry about. First, a possible impact of the imposition of the tariff is to bring down the world price of wine by curbing demand for imports; second, the revenue collected, whether it be in the form of wine or bread, must be spent in one way or another. These two complications must be accounted for as well. To allow for the first, we will assume that Europe's offer curve is not a straight line but displays some curvature. This implies, of course, that any reduction in demand for Europe's exports will have the effect of depressing their prices somewhat. The second complication, that of government demand, or of private demand if the revenue proceeds are redistributed, is taken care of by allowing the revenue to be spent partly on the home good and partly on the import good. In this way we can capture general aspects of the problem and allow for special cases to arise within the same framework.

Suppose, then, that America imposes a tariff of *PR/RS* percent on wine imports and spends part of the revenue collected on wine and the remainder on bread. The height of the tariff is taken as arbitrarily given; we are only interested for the moment in its impact on trade and foreign and domestic prices. It is immediately clear that the same trade pattern and terms of trade cannot continue to ensure equilibrium since the price of wine in America would be bid up by the amount of the tariff, thereby causing a reduction in the demand for imports. In short, the immediate impact of the tariff is to reduce American demand for wine imports from Europe. With a less than perfectly elastic offer curve, the price at which Europe offers wine will decline. We have, therefore, a tendency for the tariff-inclusive price of wine in America to rise, and a tendency for its world or European price to decline. To this, we must add the effect on world demand patterns of the expenditure of the tariff proceeds. We will simply assume that part is spent on wine, and part on bread. Thus, for equilibrium to be restored, the demand and supply patterns for wine must be equilibrated with the imposition of the tariff, and including the impact of the expenditure of the tariff proceeds. The new equilibrium satisfying these conditions is depicted in Figure 5.6.

The tariff on wine imports is *PR/RS* as a percentage of their new, lower price in Europe, which equals *TU/OU*, the slope of *OT*. The price of wine imports in America has increased to *PS/OS*, the slope of *OP*, and the number of bottles imported has contracted to *OU*. At the terms of trade depicted, there is an excess private supply of *PQ* loaves of bread and *QT* bottles of wine. These excess

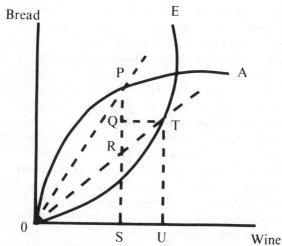

FIGURE 5–6. America Imposes a Trade Restriction. Departing from the free trade intersection, America imposes an ad valorem tariff equal to *PR/RS* on the import of wine. The resulting revenue, *PR* loaves worth of bread, is spent in the proportions *PQ* on bread and *QR* on wine by the recipients of the tariff revenue. Consequently, the price of wine has fallen to the slope of *OR*, and the domestic tariff-inclusive price of wine in America has risen to the slope of *OP*. The same trade restriction can, in principle, be brought about by an import quota of *OU* bottles of wine as long as the quota "proceeds" *PR* are spent by the recipient in the same manner as in the tariff instance.

supplies are purchased or demanded by those who spend the tariff proceeds of *PR* loaves of bread, *PQ* of which is spent on bread, and a value of *QR* loaves on wine (for example, *QT* bottles at the European price).

The new trade position is one of equilibrium with *PQ* loaves of bread going to the recipient of the tariff revenue and *QT* bottles of wine being consumed by this individual. As drawn, with both offer curves elastic, the terms of trade have worsened for Europe: it gets fewer loaves of bread per bottle exported, and the internal price of imports in America has risen. Furthermore, in terms of either good, the volume of trade has been restricted. (If Europe's offer curve were inelastic, trade in wine would increase.) *TU* loaves of bread are exported in exchange for *OU* bottles of wine.

QUOTAS

Quantitative restrictions on trade assume many forms: quotas, licensing, voluntary restraints, and health and safety requirements, to take a few examples.

In some ways such quantitative restrictions bear a close similarity to tariffs; in others they differ significantly. Consider the previous analysis of America's imposition of a tariff. The final outcome involves a lower volume of wine imports and a lower volume of bread exports. Could not this restriction of trade have been brought about in a more simple and direct manner? That is, America could simply impose a quota equal to OU on the maximum number of bottles of wine that can be imported from Europe. The quota would indeed have the effect of restricting imports to OU bottles, but is it clear that the resulting scarcity value of wine be captured by the government in the form of revenue? Not at all. For example, European wine exporters may voluntarily restrict their exports of wine by being allowed to charge the higher domestic price in America, OP, thereby capturing the excess profits of PR loaves of bread, which we can assume are spent in the same proportions as assumed above. To take a different arrangement, the government might purchase wine imports from Europe at the competitive price, the slope of OT, and simply sell all of the amount OU at that lower price to wine consumers. In this instance the revenue benefits are passed on directly to consumers. A third method of disposing of the scarcity premium would be to auction off import licenses competitively; their rental value per period would equal the difference between the domestic and foreign price (that is, PR once again), which would then go into the government coffers and could be spent on the two goods in the proportions PQ/PR and QR/PR as before. This third manner of administrating the quantitative restriction would, in principle, have the exact same real effects on domestic and foreign prices, as well as on the value of government revenue raised as the initial tariff. A fourth method of disposing of the import licenses would be to simply pass them on to friends of those in power, thereby allowing still another group to capture the scarcity premium on the restricted quantity of imports. In short, the revenue from the quota can in principle be distributed among four groups: foreign exporters, domestic importers, the government, and friends of the government. Provided that the excess profits are spent in the same way in each instance, the imposition of a quota of OU bottles of wine will have the identical real effect on prices and the volume of trade as a tariff of PR/RS percent.

Can we not therefore conclude that it makes no difference whether trade is restricted by a tariff or by a quota? No, for there is one very important difference: No matter how efficient foreigners become, they cannot export more to the quota-imposing country, whereas with a tariff it is possible for them to do so. Consider an increase in the European supply of wine exports: more wine is offered at each price ratio. In the tariff instance both the foreign and domestic prices of wine would decline, and American wine imports would increase. In the quota instance, however, the volume of wine imports is restricted to OU bottles, so that imports remain constant. Nor need the American price of wine change at all—even if the European price declines. The import demand price remains at OP for OS bottles, so that the holder of the import license, for example, can simply continue to charge the same price in America as before. Or, the price of the import titles would increase since wine imports would be cheaper for those entitled to import wine, but their price in America need not drop. We need not go into the numerous possibilities. It is clear that a quota of *OU* and its (initially) equivalent tariff *PR/RS* do not have the same dynamic consequences when foreign productivity rises. In particular, a quota serves in a sense as a method by which trade restrictions are automatically raised when foreign imports are offered at a cheaper price. For this reason, the GATT prohibits quotas.

THE METZLER AND LERNER CASES

In the previous analysis we have taken for granted that both offer curves are positively sloped at the equilibrium position; that is, that the import elasticities of demand exceed unity in both America and Europe. Lloyd Metzler (1949) explored a very interesting case in which more than the entire burden of the import tax is shifted onto the shoulders of the foreign country. As before, this must entail some significant improvement in the terms at which trade takes place; otherwise, prices are simply jacked up in America. Entirely apart from any gain due to the tariff proceeds, it is possible that the European offer curve be sufficiently inelastic so as to provoke not only a fall in the world price but also a fall in the domestic, tariff-inclusive price in America. To illustrate this possibility in the simplest way, let us assume three things: (1) the European demand for imports is inelastic or, equivalently, the European supply of exports is negatively sloped; (2) the entire tariff proceeds are spent on bread; and (3) Europe does not retaliate by erecting tariff barriers of its own. The imposition of a tariff by America under these circumstances has the effect of driving down the wine price by a percentage greater than the tariff itself, and the internal price of wine in America actually declines, despite the tariff. Figure 5–7 depicts this situation.

First, we will consider the Metzler (1949) case. At the initial trade equilibrium Europe's offer curve turns back on itself, implying that any reduction in demand for wine will induce greater supplies from Europe. With the entire proceeds of the tariff being spent on bread, the world demand pattern is further shifted away from wine, and the European and American prices decline as a result. The proceeds and expenditures of *PR* loaves of bread go, for example, to the government, and the volume of wine trade has actually increased. The price of wine in Europe, the slope of *OQ*, has fallen by a percentage greater than the tariff rate *PQ/QR*; consequently, the tariff-inclusive price in America, the slope of *OP*, is lower than at the initial trade intersection.

The Metzler case is indeed a very suggestive one: "You can have your cake and eat it, too." More wine is had—and at a cheaper price. Indeed, if the tariff proceeds are taken into account, more imports are had for less exports. Apart from the problem of retaliation, it is clear that a tariff-imposing country need not al-

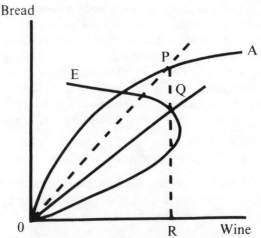

FIGURE 5-7. The Metzler and Lerner Cases. To illustrate a special example of the Metzler case, suppose that the entire tariff proceeds collected by America following the imposition of a tariff of *PQ/QR* on imports is spent on bread, the American export good. Further, since the European offer curve is inelastic, the European price of wine has fallen by a percentage greater than the tariff, so that the domestic tariff-inclusive price of wine in America has actually fallen (relative to that at the intersection of the offer curves). Now, taking the Lerner case, suppose that it is Europe that imposes the tariff but that it also spends all the tariff proceeds on bread, its import good. With inelastic domestic demand, and the expenditure of the revenue *PQ* on bread, the foreign price of bread actually rises over that at the intersection of the curves, following the imposition of the tariff.

ways suffer from its trade restrictions; it may gain. This is clear from the Organization of Petroleum Exporting Countries (OPEC) oil cartel. In fact, there is an argument that attempts to design an optimum tariff structure, to which we will turn in the next chapter.

Next consider the Lerner (1936) case. Trade restrictions are not always such a good thing for the tariff-imposing country. If we suppose in Figure 5-7 that it is Europe that imposes the tax on imports, and that the proceeds are spent entirely on bread, its import good, it is clear that Europe ends up exporting more wine, and at a lower world price (the slope of *OQ*). That is, European demand being inelastic and the expenditure of the proceeds on the import good together have the effect of worsening the tariff-imposing country's terms of trade. The exact condition for it to occur is that the proportion of the tax spent on the import good exceed the tariff-imposing country's elasticity of import demand.

INTERNATIONAL COMMODITY PRICE STABILIZATION

Frequently, governments adopt, whether in concert or individually, a trade policy designed to stabilize the price of a major export good. The international coffee and tin agreements are, theoretically, schemes of this sort. The motives for a policy of price stabilization are mixed but typically involve two elements that are difficult to separate: (1) the *stabilization* of exports of a commodity whose supply varies widely and frequently, thereby avoiding large price fluctuations, particularly if foreign demand is relatively stable and not very price elastic, and (2) the *restriction* of exports of a commodity for which foreign demand may be inelastic, thereby taking into account monopoly power on the world market. Strictly speaking, the restriction policy has more to do with keeping a price high than with price stabilization. However, the pursuit of favorable terms of trade under the guise of a price stabilization program is not uncommon. A stabilization policy has, in principle, the goal of preventing fluctuations, both upward and downward, in the world price of a commodity. In practice the policy frequently has the effect of primarily avoiding a downward movement toward a lower competitive price. So it is hard to separate the two policies, both in theory and in practice.

Graphically, we might caricature the problem in the following way (Figure 5-8). A price stabilization program for European wine exports might choose to set a relative price of PS/OS per bottle of wine exported. Notice in passing that the price chosen has (perhaps wisely) avoided exports into the inelastic portion of America's offer curve. Frequently, there are wide fluctuations in the supply of wine exports: periods of relative abundance, as characterized by the offer OE, are followed by periods of scarcity, associated with an export supply schedule OE'. The frequent fluctuations in export supplies may be the result, for example, of vagaries in the weather. Faced by fairly stable foreign demand conditions, as summarized by OA, the price of wine would change significantly from period to period in the absence of governmental intervention. During periods of abundant supply, the government might therefore intervene in private markets. During a period of abundance, it would buy up exactly ST bottles of wine, so that the European supply of exports is reduced to OS bottles, thereby maintaining the export price of PS/OS. Similarly, during periods of scarce supply characterized by a smaller offer OE', the government can sell from its accumulated stock of wine a quantity equal to RS bottles to maintain a stable, set price. Notice that a policy of price stabilization has a very simple rule of market intervention: (1) supply from government stocks any excess foreign demand at the set price when demand exceeds supply and (2) buy up any excess supply when export supplies exceed world demand.

This type of policy would be one of relatively pure price stabilization—for example, avoiding wide fluctuations in price. It may, however, serve at the same

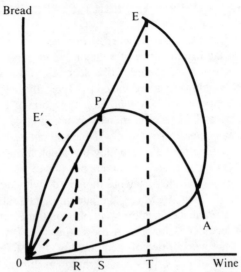

FIGURE 5–8. International Commodity Price Stabilization. Owing to the vagaries of weather, European export supplies of wine vary widely. During periods of relative scarcity, as characterized by the offer curve *OE'*, the price would tend to rise significantly, whereas during periods of relative abundance, summarized by *OE*, the price would fall off drastically. To avoid such wide fluctuations in price, European authorities purchase any excess supply of wine, *ST* bottles, for instance, during a period of abundance and sell *RS* bottles, the private excess demand on the world market during periods of scarcity. By this policy of offsetting divergences between export supply and foreign demand, a stable price of *PS/OS* loaves of bread per bottle is set. Notice that the price chosen might involve growing governmental stocks of wine, suggesting that price stabilization may also serve the purpose of export restriction.

time the purpose of keeping the average price high and, in particular, of avoiding situations in which increased export supplies earn less in terms of imports. Indeed, if the type of intervention taken by the authorities is one characterized by purchases as a rule rather than sales, and therefore growing governmental stocks, it might be more accurate to describe the policy as one of export restriction.

When the authorities use export quotas (for example, equal to *OS* bottles of wine) on either a country-by-country or firm-by-firm basis, it is frequently the case that the policy is not designed to avoid price fluctuations per se but rather to avoid a low price in general. In short, while the problem of price stabilization can in principle be treated as conceptually different from a policy of trade restriction, *stabilization* is often a euphemism for *restriction*. In general the two policies are intermingled to varying degrees by necessity since some intervention price must be chosen. If the price chosen is above the average market price, an element of restriction automatically comes into play.

THE SMALL, OPEN COUNTRY MODEL
WITH NONTRADED GOODS

Although many goods are internationally traded, some are not. Services, in particular, provide a good example of nontraded goods. It is useful for conceptual purposes to make a sharp distinction between traded and nontraded goods. Traded goods include both exports and imports, whereas nontraded goods take in all the rest. When the exchange rate, for example, is not adjusted to correspond to domestic inflation, there can be a dramatic change in the relative price of traded versus nontraded goods. When domestic inflation outspeeds exchange rate depreciation, traded goods become relatively cheap. On the other hand, when the exchange rate is depreciated abruptly, traded goods become suddenly very expensive. This section develops the Australian model of a small, open economy with nontraded goods, which we owe to Australian economist W. E. Salter (1952). Salter made a very useful simplification: When a country is small, both its export and import prices in foreign currency are fixed by world supply and demand on the world market. When the prices of two goods are fixed relative to one another, it is possible to consider them as the same good. This is Sir John Hick's (1946) composite good theorem. For example, if the world price of coffee is $3.00 a pound, whereas the price of sugar is $0.50 a pound, one-sixth pound of coffee and one pound of sugar can be considered as the same good purchased for $0.50. By an appropriate choice of units, all export and import goods may be lumped together into one composite good, which we will call the *traded good*. Similarly, we may aggregate all nontraded goods into a single category called the *nontraded good*.

During any period, an economy produces and consumes both traded and nontraded goods. In Figure 5-9 trade equilibrium is indicated at point *P,C* where production and consumption of traded goods are the same, which gives, by definition, trade equilibrium; production and consumption of nontraded goods are identical, which gives equilibrium in the market for home goods. The relative price of traded to nontraded goods is indicated by the slope of the line passing through *P,C.*

It is useful to introduce here the notion of *domestic absorption. Absorption* refers to the total quantity of goods and services consumed by domestic entities: consumers, investors, and the government. When domestic absorption exceeds domestic production, the economy runs a trade deficit that is financed either by foreign lending or by drawing down upon the central bank's foreign reserves. Since the production of nontraded goods equals their consumption, the value of the trade deficit equals the consumption of traded goods minus their production. (See Figure 5-10.)

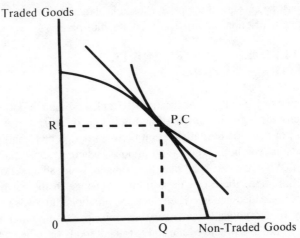

FIGURE 5–9. Trade Equilibrium with Nontraded Goods. Production and consumption of both traded and nontraded goods are in equilibrium at point P,C. The vertical distance QP represents both production and consumption of traded goods. When the volume produced and consumed of traded goods is the same, there is trade balance. The slope of the line passing through P,C gives the price of nontraded goods in terms of traded goods.

Suppose, for instance, that the initial equilibrium point P,C is disturbed by an exogenous increase in the money supply by fiat. The excess cash balances will induce a generalized increase in expenditure on both traded and nontraded goods. Consequently, the expenditure line initially shifts outward parallel to the income line passing through P,C, portraying the fact that expenditure exceeds income as individuals attempt to rid themselves of excess liquidity. The nominal price of traded goods remains fixed with a fixed exchange rate, but the excess demand for nontraded goods results in a rise in their price. In addition, therefore, the relative price line becomes steeper as nontraded goods become relatively more expensive. Thus, during the adjustment process a consumption point C' and a production point P' may represent a temporary equilibrium. The value of the deficit induced by the exogenous increase in the money supply equals the distance $P'C'$, and the money price of nontraded goods adjusts so as to maintain equilibrium in the market.

As the process of adjustment wears on, the deficit causes money to flow out and the expenditure line to contract toward its initial position, since both expenditure and the nominal price of nontraded goods must ultimately decline. To avoid the ultimate deflation in the nontraded goods sector, a devaluation would simultaneously reduce expenditure via the liquidity effect and switch demand toward nontraded goods via the substitution effect. The liquidity and substitution effects taken together tend to contract the expenditure line passing through C' and lower

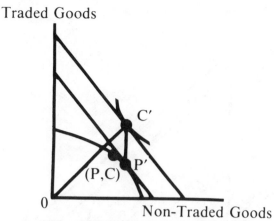

Traded Goods

Non-Traded Goods

FIGURE 5-10.   An Increase in the Money Supply or Foreign Borrowing. An increase in domestic expenditure financed by an increase in either the money supply or foreign borrowing causes domestic absorption to rise relative to domestic production, resulting in a trade deficit equal to $P'C'$, and a rise in the relative price of home goods under a fixed exchange rate system. A currency devaluation would directly reduce absorption by taxing domestic cash balances and reducing real wages (if they are not fully indexed) and would raise the relative price of traded goods, thereby switching expenditure onto home goods. Both effects would move the economy back toward equilibrium at P,C.

its slope, thereby moving toward the initial equilibrium P,C with a lower price of nontraded goods. In addition to devaluation, other policies to reduce absorption relative to production are reductions in government spending and/or tax increases, which both act directly on absorption. Indeed, it is nowadays commonplace for the International Monetary Fund (IMF) also to set targets for the government deficit—for example, government expenditure minus taxes—since the government budget deficit is a major source of money creation. This is so because a budget deficit must be financed either by new borrowing or by new issue of money by the central bank. Money growth, then, can be restrained by reduction of the budget deficit.

Finally, it should be noted in the current context of debt crisis in Latin America and Africa that debt repayment requires that the debtor countries reduce absorption below production to generate the trade surpluses necessary to repay foreign debt (see Figure 5-11). Obviously, this entails a global reduction in the standard of living in these countries, which is already low by U.S. and European standards. Clearly, this has jeopardized the political stability of a number of countries. So far, Mexico has astounded many by dampening absorption sufficiently under their IMF program to generate a trade surplus in a year. At the same time, large-scale unemployment has been avoided thanks to downwardly

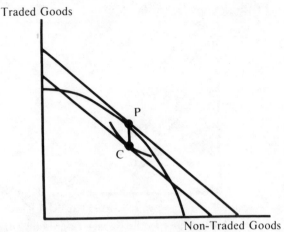

Traded Goods

Non-Traded Goods

FIGURE 5-11. The Debtor's Quandary. In order to repay debt, a country must, by definition, reduce domestic absorption relative to production to generate the trade surplus *PC* necessary for debt repayment. This requires a reduction in the standard of living and possibly political instability. Further, policies to restrict absorption also tend to restrict production.

flexible real wages, which have fallen a full one fourth since the inception of the program. These results could not have been achieved if Mexico did not have a long tradition of democratic political stability. It is not surprising that the fragile democracy just elected in Argentina is among the first to resist debt repayment.

CONCLUSION

The Marshallian offer curve is a powerful apparatus for analyzing trade problems such as equilibrium, stability, and commercial policy. We have seen that a tariff typically causes a higher relative price of imports in the home market and a lower relative price of the import good on the world market. In addition, a quota on imports has the identical static effects of a tariff but restricts trade more when there are dynamic changes abroad that lead to an increased offer of imports.

International commodity price stabilization by the purchase and sale of a good at a fixed price was analyzed by the use of offer curves. Finally, we introduced a nontraded goods sector and focused upon the balance of trade as the difference between domestic production and domestic absorption. The importance of the role of the relative price of nontraded goods is highlighted. In particular the price of home goods rises relative to international goods when domestic credit policy is more expansionary than the rate of exchange rate depreciation. Adjustment may require more rapid exchange rate depreciation and a reduction in absorption relative to production.

SELECTED READINGS

Bhagwati, Jagdish, and T. N. Srinivassan. 1971. "Trade Policy and Development." In *International Economic Policy,* edited by R. Dornbusch and J. Frenkel. Baltimore: Johns Hopkins Press.

Bhagwati, Jagdish, and Harry Johnson. 1960. "Notes on Some Controversies in the Theory of International Trade." *Economic Journal* (March).

Connolly, Michael, and Dean Taylor. 1976. "Adjustment to Devaluation with Money and Non-Traded Goods." *Journal of International Economics* 5 (August).

Dornbusch, Rudiger. 1974. "Real and Monetary Aspects of the Effects of Exchange Rate Change," In *National Monetary Policies and the International Financial System,* edited by R. Z. Aliber. Chicago: University of Chicago Press.

Hicks, John R. 1946. *Value and Capital,* Oxford: Clarendon Press.

Leontief, Wassily. 1933. "The Use of Indifference Curves in the Analysis of Foreign Trade." *Quarterly Journal of Economics* (May).

Lerner, Abba. 1936. "Symmetry between Import and Export Taxes." *Economica* (August).

Meade, James. 1952. *A Geometry of International Trade,* London: Allen & Unwin.

Metzler, Lloyd. 1949. "Tariffs, the Terms of Trade and the Distribution of National Income." *Journal of Political Economy* (February).

Mundell, Robert. 1960. "The Pure Theory of International Trade." *American Economic Review* (March).

Newberry, D., and J. Stiglitz. 1981. *The Theory of Commodity Price Stabilization.* Oxford: At the University Press.

Salter, W. E. 1952. "Internal and External Balance: The Role of Price and Expenditure Effects." *Economic Record* 35.

Tanzi, V., and M. Blejer. 1983. "Fiscal Deficits and Balance of Payments Disequilibrium in IMF Adjustment Programs." *Adjustment, Conditionality and International Financing.* Washington, D.C.: International Monetary Fund.

SIX

TARIFFS AND QUOTAS: WELFARE ASPECTS

From the vantage of the world taken as a whole, any tariff or trade restriction is not Pareto optimal. That is, a country can be persuaded to remove its trade restriction, and all countries potentially gain in the process of trade liberalization. From the standpoint of an individual country taken in isolation, however, it may gain by imposing an optimal tariff designed to improve its terms of trade. But, other countries stand to lose in this case. Perhaps the most glaring example of the aggressive use of trade restrictions to take advantage of monopoly power in the 1970s has been the oil cartel, that is, OPEC. This chapter takes up the analysis of the so-called optimum tariff, which seeks nationalistic gain at the expense of other countries. It derives the elasticity condition—namely, the optimum tariff equals the reciprocal of the foreign elasticity of supply—and analyzes the consequences of foreign retaliation.

The final part of the chapter examines various well-known arguments for protection such as the infant industry argument and the domestic unemployment argument. The chapter concludes with a short discussion of the theory of effective protection when a final good uses imported inputs and the tariff rates on the inputs differ from the tariff rates on the final good.

TARIFFS AND WORLD WELFARE

If America imposes a tariff on wine imports that is not completely prohibitive, the domestic relative price of imports faced by consumers in America will exceed the price abroad by the percentage amount of the tariff. Since it is in the best interests of both consumers and producers in each country to equate their respective rates of substitution in consumption and production with the relative prices they face, and since these prices differ by the amount of the tariff, it follows that the production and consumption efficiency requirements are not satisfied. That is to say, opportunity costs in production differ, implying that the production blocks intersect, as do rates of exchange in consumption, suggesting that the indifference curves also intersect. Within each country, the marginal rates of substitution in consumption and production are equal; the problem is that they are not the same in America and Europe. This situation is depicted in Figure 6-1.

The slope of the line ii' represents prices in Europe, and the slope of the parallel lines mm' and nn' indicates the price in America, the percentage differences being equal to the tariff. Trade is in equilibrium since the quantity of exports that each country offers is readily absorbed abroad at the prices that reign there. In other words the production pattern P' and consumption pattern R' are consistent ones. The domestic equality of rates of exchange in production and consumption with prices at home is reflected in the tangency of America's production frontier and consumption indifference curve to the lines mm' and nn', respectively, and those of Europe to ii'. Thus, while the rates of exchange in production and consumption within each country are the same, they differ from country to country because of the tariff, and therein lies the inefficiency. It should also be clear that what we have with a tariff, in effect, is a tax on the consumption of the import good and a subsidy to its production. Indeed, it is entirely feasible to duplicate a tariff by taxing the consumption of an import good and giving the proceeds to domestic import-competing producers. Since the percentage premium is the same with an equal ad valorem tax on consumption and subsidy to production, effective changes in trade policy can be brought about by internal taxes and subsidies. Note once again that the benchmark of what we have in mind is the world one: the inability to benefit one country at no expense to the other. But this does not mean that America is worse off owing to the tariff; rather, it means that if it benefits by protection, it is at the expense of Europe. In this sense the burden of the tariff may be shifted onto Europe. This shift comes about through the worsening of Europe's terms of trade—its exports now earn less in terms of its imports.

In addition to the risk of foreign retaliation, two considerations—the volume of trade and the terms of trade—must be weighed against one another by America in imposing the tariff because the reduction in volume mitigates against the gains due to the improvement in terms. There is an argument for protection known as the optimum tariff one that takes these two elements into account. The so-called optimum tariff is that one that puts the home country onto its highest indifference curve, subject to the condition that trade must balance. Essentially, the home country exploits its monopoly power, the ability to influence the terms of trade, in the most efficient manner; and this restriction on trade may be worthwhile even if tariff retaliation by the foreign country takes place. The optimum tariff argument goes something like this. Unrestricted trade tends to equate domestic rates of exchange in production and consumption with foreign prices. This is brought about by the atomistic actions of producers and consumers who go about doing the best they can as though they had no influence on prices. And

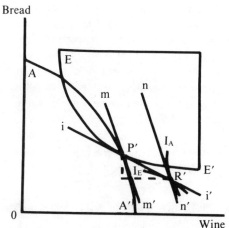

FIGURE 6–1. Tariff in America. A tariff has the effect of introducing a gap between domestic and foreign prices. The European relative price of wine is indicated by the slope of *ii′*, and the domestic American price, inclusive of the tariff, by the slope of the parallel lines *mm′* and *nn′*. In each country producers and consumers behave so as to equate their marginal rates of exchange in production and consumption with relative prices. It follows that these rates must differ in America and Europe. This is depicted by the intersection of both the production frontiers at *P′* and the social indifference curves at *R′*. Consequently, both production and consumption inefficiency is the outcome.

for each one taken separately, this may be entirely true. But for all taken together, it is definitely not. In particular, prices depend on—among other things—the volume of trade. The more imports, the higher their price; the more exports, the lower their price. But this is really the same thing, for exports must exactly pay for imports at their relative price if trade is to balance. In other words it is the terms of trade that count. Furthermore, the terms of trade depend upon the volume of trade. So by restricting the volume of trade, a country can improve the terms on which it takes place. But it must not go too far; the improvement is likely to be of little value if the volume has shrunk out of proportion. The optimum tariff argument balances the two against each other. From this point of view, the term *optimum tariff* is an unfortunate one. For what it really has to do with is an optimal restriction on trade. If we wish to be pedantic about it, we would insist that the restriction be called an *optimum tax on trade,* at best, rather than an *optimum tariff.*

OPTIMUM TARIFF

Let us see how we would go about finding what an optimum tariff for America might look like. As America's imports of wine rise, so does their price.

As a buyer America should take this into account because an extra unit of wine through imports costs more than just its price since the price is raised on all units imported. What is, then, the total cost of an extra bottle of wine obtained from abroad? Clearly, it is the price plus something that depends upon the volume of imports. To be exact, this extra cost can be measured by the rise in the price per bottle of extra imports times the total number of bottles imported. In short, the cost of obtaining an extra bottle of wine through foreign trade can be stated precisely as

$$p + \frac{\partial p}{\partial Y}\ Y,$$

where p is the foreign relative price of wine, $\frac{\partial p}{\partial Y}$ is the change in the price per bottle of extra imports, and Y is the total quantity of imports. This can be expressed in terms of the elasticity of supply of imports, ϵ—the percentage change in supply divided by the percentage change in price as $p(1 + 1/\epsilon)$. This latter expression measures marginal import cost and indicates the toal amount of bread that must be exported in order to acquire an extra bottle of wine from abroad. It exceeds price whenever the elasticity of supply is positive but less than infinity—in other words, whenever the country has some ability to influence prices.

Extra bottles of wine can also be obtained from domestic sources. Namely, production of wine can be expanded at the expense of production of bread. The precise cost of acquiring extra bread by this route is indicated by the slope of the domestic production frontier. This slope, the marginal rate of transformation, measures the extra sacrifice of bread necessary to produce more wine at home. We thus have two routes by which to get more wine. It is clear that if one were cheaper than the other, it would pay to acquire more by the cheaper method and less by the more expensive one. This is neither more nor less than the self-evident proposition that saving results when something is obtained at a lower price. Here, however, the point is that the total cost to the economy of an extra import is composed of two elements: (1) the price (2) plus the rise in price times the quantity imported. It is also evident that no further savings can be had when the two routes, domestic and foreign, cost exactly the same. Indeed, the optimum tariff is designed to bring this about. But one last step remains in the argument. That is, perfect competition brings into equality domestic prices and the opportunity costs in production and exchange at home. We can therefore measure the marginal cost of obtaining bread from domestic sources by its domestic price, which we indicate by π. Since bread is imported, we also know that the domestic price exceeds the foreign one by a percentage equal to tariff, which we indicate by t. That is, $\pi = p\,(1 + t)$. This is true of all tariffs— not only an optimum one. For the tariff to be optimal it must bring into equality the domestic opportunity cost, π, and the marginal import cost, $p\,(1+1/\epsilon)$. Obviously, the requirement $P\,(1+t)=P\,(1+1/\epsilon)$ is satisfied by a tariff equal to the reciprocal of the foreign elasticity of supply of imports. This is an entirely plausible result. The foreign elasticity of supply is an index of the degree of monopoly power that America exerts. The higher the foreign elasticity, the lower the monopoly power. Accordingly, the higher the elasticity, the lower the optimum tariff.

As the ability to influence foreign prices disappears (the elasticity approaches infinity), the optimum tariff approaches zero. This means that if America cannot improve its terms of trade—for instance, it is a small country—America is better off without tariffs.

However, the optimum tariff could never be negative (for example, an import subsidy), for this would imply a negative elasticity of foreign supply. If this were true, more imports could be had for fewer exports by an increase in the tariff. This follows because a negative elasticity means that the import supply curve has a negative slope (the foreign offer curve turns back on itself). So logically the optimum tariff formula $t=1/\epsilon$ applies only in the range of positive foreign elasticity, a higher tariff being the best policy in the range of negative elasticity. Before going further, let us make clear the sense in which a tariff strategy is said to be optimal. The argument has been couched in terms of finding the most efficient way of obtaining additional quantities of an import good. We saw that if one route were cheaper than the other, as is the case of free trade when the home country has some monopoly power, savings can be had. Further, these savings are in terms of other goods, for this is how we have measured costs. To put the matter bluntly, the optimum tariff strategy is designed to guarantee to the home country the greatest possible consumption of bread for any given level of consumption of wine. This ensures that it is not possible to make any one citizen better off at no expense to others. In other words the tariff policy we have just outlined is optimal in the Pareto sense for a country acting in isolation. It is not Pareto optimal for all countries taken together, because any tariff, including the optimum one, fails to satisfy the world Pareto efficiency conditions. A graph might help drive this point home—see Figure 6–2.

Point P in Figure 6–2 represents one possible efficient production pattern in America. Suppose trade takes place from this point, Europe offering wine in exchange for bread on terms depicted by its offer curve *PE*, drawn from *P* as the origin of trade. In principle, America may choose any pattern of trade characterized by a point on *E*'s offer curve, for along it trade will be in balance. However, the optimum tariff argument seeks out an efficient pattern. As we have seen, this requires that domestic and foreign routes to obtaining additional bread entail the same sacrifice. That is to say, equality of the marginal rate of transformation in production with the marginal import costs (marginal rate of transformation through trade) is the criterion for efficiency. Since the former is the slope of the production frontier and the latter is the slope of Europe's offer curve, a

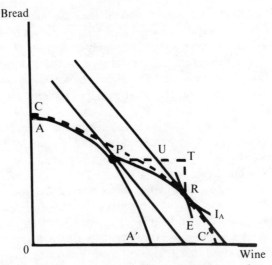

Bread

Wine

FIGURE 6–2. The Optimum Tariff. In the absence of retaliation an optimum tariff is one that brings into equality the domestic marginal rate of exchange with the foreign marginal rate of exchange. If the home country has any monopoly power, the import price rises with the volume of imports, so that marginal import cost exceeds the import price. An optimum tariff policy requires, therefore, that the slope of the domestic production frontier at any point such as P equal the slope of the (inverted) foreign offer curve at R. By taking all such points that satisfy this equality of marginal rates, we trace out a consumption frontier CC' known as the Baldwin envelope, which indicates the maximum feasible consumption set attainable by an optimum tariff. Since the foreign price of imported wine is TR/PT, and the domestic price is TR/UT, the optimum tariff equals the percentage difference, PU/UT. Since PU/UT is the reciprocal of the foreign elasticity of supply, an optimum tariff policy requires a tariff equal to the reciprocal of the foreign elasticity of supply.

point on the offer curve having the same slope as the production frontier at point P will satisfy this criterion. R is such a point, the line tangent to it being parallel to the line tangent to P. America's optimum tariff strategy is designed to make point R a possible consumption point through trade. It clearly could not come about by free trade because the accompanying terms of trade (the slope of the line TR/PT) differ from the domestic opportunity costs (the slope of the line tangent to P, or TR/UT, since the line through UR is parallel to the line through P). However, an optimum tariff, by driving an appropriate wedge between domestic and foreign prices, can bring this about. How can we measure this optimal wedge graphically? Recalling that the basic relationship between domestic and foreign relative prices is $\pi = p\,(1+t)$, we have

$$\pi = \frac{TR}{UT} \quad \text{and} \quad p = \frac{TR}{PT},$$

so

$$\frac{TR}{UT} = \frac{TR}{PT}(1+t)$$

$$1+t = \frac{PT}{UT}$$

$$t = \frac{PT}{UT} - 1 = \frac{PT - UT}{UT} = \frac{PU}{UT}$$

$$= \frac{1}{\dfrac{UT}{PU}} = \frac{1}{\epsilon},$$

the reciprocal of the foreign elasticity of supply. It can be measured alternatively as $1/(PT/PU-1)=(1/\eta-1)$, the reciprocal of the foreign elasticity of demand minus one. This follows from John Stuart Mill's principle of reciprocal demand as embodied in an offer curve.

By using a little algebra, the optimum tax formula can be expressed in an interesting way. Note first that America's wine imports, I, equal European production of wine, Y, less European consumption y, or $I=Y-y$. Furthermore, both production and consumption of bread in Europe depend upon its relative price, p, or: $Y=Y(p)$ and $y=y(p)$. We may differentiate Europe's export equation with respect to the price of bread and divide by p/I to obtain

$$\frac{p}{I}\frac{\partial I}{\partial p} = \frac{Y}{I}\frac{p}{Y}\frac{\partial Y}{\partial p} - \frac{y}{I}\frac{p}{y}\frac{\partial y}{\partial p},$$

or equivalently,

$$\epsilon_{IP} = \frac{Y}{I}\epsilon_{Yp} + \frac{y}{I}\epsilon_{yp}. \tag{6.1}$$

That is, the foreign elasticity of supply of exports equals a weighted sum of the foreign elasticities of production supply and consumption demand. Furthermore, let us define μ as I/Y the proportion of European wine production that is exported.

Making use of this relationship in equation 6.1, we can express the optimum tax formula as its reciprocal:

$$t = \frac{1}{\frac{1}{\mu} \epsilon_{Yp} + \left(\frac{1}{\mu} - 1 \right) \epsilon_{yp}}. \tag{6.2}$$

So the optimum tax on imports depends on three factors: imports as a proportion of foreign production, the foreign elasticity of production supply, and the elasticity of consumption demand abroad for the export good. In particular, holding the other variables in the formula constant, we can say that the optimum tax is *greater* (1) the larger imports are as a proportion of foreign production, (2) the smaller the elasticity of foreign production supply, and (3) the lower the foreign elasticity of consumption demand for their export good.

It would seem that the picture is now complete. But it really is not because there is no reason to believe that point R is a desirable one to reach. It is the efficient consumption possibility corresponding to production point P. But we have chosen the latter in a completely arbitrary fashion. Does this cast doubt on the optimum tariff argument? No, on the contrary, for we could choose any other production point on America's production frontier and, in a similar manner, find the corresponding efficient consumption point attainable through foreign trade. The essence of the argument is that an optimum tariff is the suitable policy for all such situations. To see this, we slide Europe's offer curve along America's production frontier $AA,'$, which serves as a locus of origins, to find all efficient consumption points by the rule of equality of slopes.

These consumption points trace out, in turn, a curve termed the *Baldwin envelope* after its originator Robert Baldwin (1948) that serves as a consumption possibility frontier, CC', indicating the maximum possible consumption of one good for each level of consumption of the other. It follows that along CC' it is not possible to make any resident of America better off at no expense to any other. In other words, points on CC' are Pareto efficent for America. An optimum tariff policy is necessary to land America on this curve, no matter which consumption point is chosen, and a tariff equal to the reciprocal of the foreign elasticity of supply measured from the point chosen will accomplish this.

Putting the optimum tariff argument in terms of a consumption possibility frontier has the advantage of making clear that its validity does not hinge in any way upon the supposed existence of a well-behaved social welfare index. We have, so to speak, skirted the matter of choosing a favored consumption point on the CC' frontier simply becuase it has not been necessary to the argument. It may, however, be very convenient to do so—particularly when it is not possible to make use of domestic opportunity costs in setting up the argument. Suppose, for instance, that the production pattern P were rigidly fixed so that wine cannot be transformed into bread domestically. This could arise if, for one reason or another, factors of production could not move from one industry to the other. Under these circumstances it makes no sense to speak of the domestic marginal rate of transformation since the production possibility frontier shrinks to point P. But we have until now phrased the optimum tariff argument in terms of equating domestic opportunity costs of production with marginal rates of exchange through foreign trade. Does the argument therefore falter if the goods cannot be transformed into one another at home? The answer is no, because domestic prices can still be used to evaluate the relative domestic worth of the goods, at least under broadly competitive conditions. This is so because the goods are still exchanged for one another domestically, and optimal consumption behavior requires that each individual equate his or her marginal rate of substitution in consumption to the relative price that person faces.

This implies that domestic prices continue to play the role of reflecting the relative worth of goods to the home country. The optimum tariff argument loses none of its force; rather, it involves equating the marginal rates of transformation through foreign trade with consumers' marginal rates of substitution in consumption. The optimum tariff argument still holds for the common-sense reason that a country, like a buyer or seller, might turn the terms of trade in its favor by restricting its purchases. The best a trader could do would be to put himself or herself on the highest indifference curve, subject to the condition that sales pay for purchases. The individual would select a point on the opposing offer curve, such as R, tangent to his or her indifference curve. We have done the same thing for a country because relative prices reflect rates of substitution in consumption. For this reason it does not seem entirely implausible to say that at point R the social rate of indifference equals the private rate, so that we can go ahead and sketch in a social indifference curve tangent to R. In short, a tariff is optimal because it takes into account domestic consumers' collective monopoly power in their foreign purchases. Graphically, this monopoly is reflected in the curvature of the foreign offer curve, giving rise to a distinction between the average terms of trade, $\dfrac{TR}{PT}$, and the marginal terms of trade, $\dfrac{TR}{UT}$.

Putting in the domestic social indifference curve, I_A, completes the picture. Desired exports TR and imports PT exactly cancel each other at the terms of trade, so that trade balances. The total value of expenditure in America exceeds the total value of production at world prices by the amount of the tariff revenue, PU.

SYMMETRY OF EXPORT AND IMPORT TAXES

At this point it might be appropriate to recall that the optimum tariff argument can be expressed entirely in terms of an optimum tax restriction on exports designed to improve the terms of trade. If trade is to balance, a restriction on exports entails an equal restriction in the value of imports. What we are really talking about is an optimal restriction on trade; a tax on exports has the same real effects as an equal tax on imports. Both create the same divergence between foreign and domestic price ratios. Consider a tariff, for instance, causing a domestic premium on imports; their domestic relative price exceeds the foreign one by the percentage amount of the tariff. However, since it is only relative prices that count here, this means that the foreign price of the export good exceeds its domestic price by the same percentage premium. But this is exactly what would result if an equal tax on exports had been imposed rather than a tariff. Furthermore, with trade in balance both would raise the same revenue. Therefore, provided that the proceeds are disposed of in the same manner in both instances, we need not distinguish between taxes on exports and imports, but rather we can speak solely in terms of a restriction on trade. In short, it is trade that is taxed, not imports. This important point is frequently overlooked. It is not, however, lost on everyone; exporters are typically among the most vocal in opposing restrictions on imports. They may also fear foreign retaliation, of course.

To put the symmetry argument in terms of offer curves, in Figure 6–3 the percentage import tariff is PR/RS, which equals PU/UO by similar triangles. In turn, PU/UO equals RU/UT, once again by similar triangles, which implies that an export tax of RU/UT would have the identical real effects on trade and relative prices, provided that the tariff proceeds are spent in the same manner in both instances—that is, PQ is spent on bread, and QR is spent on wine.

This symmetry implies that the optimum tariff argument can be phrased entirely in terms of an optimum tax on exports designed to make traders take into account marginal export revenue, rather than the foreign price of exports. One can speak indifferently of marginal import cost exceeding the price of imports, or of marginal export revenue falling short of the price of exports. In both instances the price is a relative one, the terms of trade, so that they are identical ways of expressing the same thing. To make sure this point is clear, we can briefly derive that optimum tax on trade by the export route. Returning to Figure 6–2, the optimum tariff, marginal export revenue (the additional imports of wine obtainable as a proportion of extra exports of bread) at point R is indicated by TU/TR, the slope of the foreign offer curve. It falls short of the foreign price of exports at R, PT/TR, because the latter declines as exports rise. By exactly how much do they differ? Note that marginal export revenue equals

$$\frac{TU}{TR} = \frac{PT - PU}{TR} = \frac{PT}{TR}\left(1 - \frac{PU}{PT}\right) = \frac{1}{p}\left(1 - \frac{1}{\eta}\right).$$

That is, marginal export revenue falls short of the foreign price of bread (the reciprocal of the foreign price of wine) by 100 $1/\eta$ percent of the foreign price, where η equals Europe's elasticity of demand for imports of bread. Hence, an

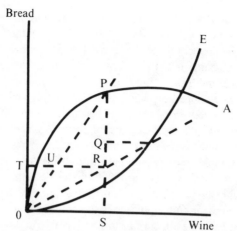

FIGURE 6-3. The Symmetry of Export and Import Taxes. In a two-good world a tax on imports has the identical effect of a tax on exports, provided that the revenue proceeds are spent in the same manner. The tariff on imports is $PR/RS=PU/UO=RU/UT$, which in turn would be the tax on exports having the equivalent effect on the volume and terms of trade. This holds so long as PQ of the revenue PR is spent on bread, and QR is spent on wine in each case. In short, it is trade that is taxed, not imports.

ad valorem tax on exports of $1/\eta$ as a percentage of the foreign price would bring into equality domestic and foreign marginal rates of exchange. The optimum export tax, as a proportion of their foreign price, is equal to $PU/PT=1/\eta$, the reciprocal of the foreign elasticity of the demand for imports. As a proportion of the domestic price of the exportable good, the optimal tax on exports is equal to PU/UT, the reciprocal of the foreign elasticity of supply of exports. Thus we have arrived at exactly the same result.

TARIFFS AND RETALIATION

Before passing on to other trade problems, it is important to put the optimum tariff argument into proper perspective. One thing that it does not show is that a country is always better off in restricting trade in view of improving the terms on which it takes place, even if it does so in a so-called optimal manner. For one thing other countries may retaliate with similar tariff restrictions. If so, the home country may end up worse off than it was to begin with.

In one sense not much can be said when we open up the possibility of foreign retaliation, for then we enter the complicated realm of game theory and optimal strategies. The problem is not so much that two countries play a tariff game; rather, it is that the game is not a strictly competitive one. What one country gains does not equal the losses of the other, as in a game of poker. Both countries stand to gain by cooperating instead of by erecting tariff barriers. This is so because barriers to trade bring about inefficiencies in consumption and production patterns; consequently, their elimination leads to greater production possibilities, and both countries can share in the gains.

To take an example, Europe could afford to bribe America to dismantle its tariff, whether it is an optimal one or not, and still be better off. In short, free trade solutions with the possibility of transfers of income are always superior from the point of view of both countries concerned to any impediments to trade such as tariffs that have the effect of distorting relative prices. In technical terms Pareto efficient solutions dominate others. But this does not necessarily get us very far because we cannot be sure which Pareto efficient solution is the one actually contracted. The outcome is typically indeterminate. Another problem is that the theory either assumes or predicts that tariffs, quotas, and other restrictions to trade cannot come about since they are inefficient. This does not square too well with the fact that almost all countries have elaborate restrictions on trade that—despite lengthy negotation—cannot seem to be entirely done away with.

One game theory solution does exist that allows for the existence of tariffs in the final outcome. The idea originated with Harry Johnson (1953–54) and is based upon Cournot behavioral assumptions: namely, that each country retaliates to changes in the other's tariff by imposing in turn an optimum tariff on the assumption that the other country will not retaliate. As is typical of Cournot solutions, and the shortsighted behavior implied by them, the outcome involves tariff reaction curves where retaliation is the rule and not the exception. Nevertheless, tariffs are not done away with, and the propositions developed by Johnson merit summarizing:

1. Tariff cycles may emerge, so that the retaliation sequence may go on endlessly.
2. If a stable outcome is reached, either both countries are worse off than at free trade or one country benefits but only at the expense of the other.
3. The outcome depends on which country initiates the tariff retaliation sequence.
4. It is not always best to be the first country to initiate the imposition of tariffs; the reacting country may be better off in the final outcome.
5. An optimal retaliation may involve a lowering of tariff barriers.
6. Trade will not come to an end.

STATE TRADING

In the earlier literature on international trade, it was common to treat along with the optimum tariff a possibility of making an all-or-none offer of the foreign country export good on a take-it-or-leave-it basis. This type of trade typified the economic policy of Fascist Germany. To have a flavor of the type of arrangement involved, consider Tibor Scitovsky's 1942 remarks on the subject:

> Barter trade agreements not only set the terms on which indefinite amounts of goods are to be traded for each other, but also fix the exact amounts to be exchanged. They have been introduced by Nazi Germany in her trade with South American and South-East European countries, and declared by a Nazi spokesman to be the principle on which trade in Hitler's "New Order" would be based. [P. 378, Ellis and Metzler]

He then "sets out to prove that barter agreements may be to the mutual advantage of countries whose trade was previously conducted across tariff walls: but that at the same time they are a convenient way of exacting tribute from conquered or intimidated countries." Nowadays, state trading between the Soviet Union and the Eastern bloc is commonplace.

Sometimes the problem is treated under the rubric of state trading in which one country makes an offer of a precise number of exports in exchange for a specified number of imports. In other words the exchange bargain made specifies both the price and the quantity traded rather than taking account of the price alone. This section briefly outlines the all-or-none offer. The precise situation to be considered is a somewhat contrived one: the home country has perfect knowledge of the foreign country's taste and production patterns, and it makes an aggressive sort of all-or-none offer, which is accepted in a passive manner by the foreign country since it is neither better off nor worse off in doing so. We do not claim that this is the best sort of game theory, since there exists a basic asymmetry of behavior—namely, that the home country can, by its aggressive policy, extract all the gains from economic relations with foreigners, which in turn are left no better off than at autarky. The consumption possibilities available by the all-or-none offer by, say, America must therefore be superior to those attainable by the optimum tariff. As with the optimum tariff, we take the foreign country's autarkic indifference schedule depicting those combinations of imports and exports that leave Europe totally indifferent to whether or not it trades at all. Knowing those combinations of imports and exports that leave Europe no better off than without trade, we can slide this indifference curve along America's production possibility frontier and draw an envelope along which the foreign indifference curve and domestic production frontier have the same slope. Doing so, we trace out a set of consumption possibilities attainable by the all-or-none price and quantity bargain, CC', as shown in Figure 6–4.

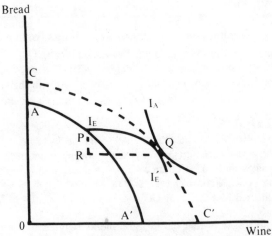

FIGURE 6–4. The All-or-None Offer. By inverting Europe's autarkic indifference curve, $I_E I'_E$, sliding it along America's production frontier, AA', and tracing the envelope of the resulting points, the consumption possibility curve CC' available to America by making an all-or-none price and quantity trade offer is derived. The derivation is identical to that of the optimum tariff with the sole exception that the autarkic indifference curve replaces the foreign offer curve. Since the former must show greater exports for each level of imports, the consumption possibilities available by an all-or-none offer are superior to those attainable by an optimum tariff policy. The other country need not, of course, accept this offer.

The optimum point on the consumption possibility frontier (formally an envelope) is indicated by the tangency of America's highest indifference curve. The corresponding all-or-none offer is RQ bottles of wine in exchange for PR loaves of bread on a take-it-or-leave-it basis. Europe accepts the offer, not being made worse off in doing so. The entire gains to trade have been realized by America. And because the autarkic indifference curve must indicate more exports for any given amount of imports than an offer curve, the all-or-none offer allows a superior consumption possibility set to America than would an optimum tariff policy.

TARIFFS AND UNEMPLOYMENT

As we have seen, international trade can be a mixed blessing: while it provides import goods at a lower opportunity cost, trade may also cause unemployment in the import-competing industry. Unemployment may result, for example, from downwardly rigid real wages of the factor intensive to the import-competing industry. It is not surprising, then, that unemployment caused by sharp rises in imports is often a major argument put forth in favor of tariff protection. Figure 6–5 illustrates a case in which a country is worse off with trade than with no trade. Point R corresponds to a posttrade output pattern with unemployment in the wine industry as a result of rigid real wages. At world prices, indicated by the slope of the line through R, the country does not have sufficient income to purchase what was previously produced at Q with no trade. Clearly then, a prohibitive tariff returning the country to autarky at Q would be superior to trade and unemployment. A less-than-prohibitive tariff that prevents the output of wine from falling so drastically such as at point S with trade at the world price ratio would be a superior policy. Some gains to trade would be realized, whereas the import-competing industry would be partially protected. That is, a consumption point such as T could be attained. The optimal policy, however, would be a direct production subsidy to the wine industry, thus avoiding the consumption tax implicit in a tariff. Production at S, for example, could be reached, and consumption at V, reflecting greater wine imports and higher consumer welfare.

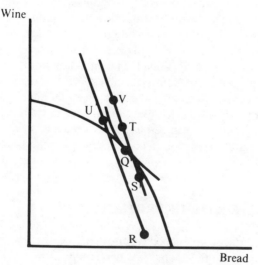

FIGURE 6–5. Tariffs and Unemployment. Trade with rigid real wages in the wine industry results in unemployment in America. Production following trade takes place at R, and consumption occurs at some point such as U along RU. The country is worse off than without trade at Q. A partial tariff restricting imports somewhat may result in a production point such as S, giving protection to the industry, and a consumption point such as T, which is superior to free trade. A production subsidy to the wine industry could maintain production at S, allowing greater wine imports and a higher welfare at consumption point V.

THE INFANT INDUSTRY ARGUMENT FOR PROTECTION

Temporary protection is sometimes called for in the case of an "infant industry" that needs to be shielded from foreign competition during its early years. This argument for protection is complex since it is, in practice, hard to identify industries that fully qualify for such protection. Suppose, for example, a new industry must sustain losses for a number of years before turning profitable. If the discounted profits outweigh present losses, a competitive economy would go ahead and invest in the industry. Unless there is some capital market imperfection, entrepreneurs would borrow and ultimately survive without protection. Another possibility for invoking protection exists: it may be that the necessary apprenticeship or "learning-by-doing" involves technological externalities that cannot be captured by the firm or industry. In this case the firm must pay a competitive wage that includes the value of the on-the-job training. Protection is also sometimes warranted in this case of technological externalities. The appropriate form of protection is a direct production subsidy to the infant industry since there is no need to tax consumption of the product indirectly.

Figure 6–6a illustrates the short-term losses incurred by tariff protection to the computer industry, whereas Figure 6–6b illustrates an outward shift in the production frontier as a result of technical progress in the computer industry, which permits domestic production to be sufficiently efficient so as not to need further protection. Production takes place at P^* and consumption at C^*. Note that an important necessary condition for infant industry protection to have been a good investment is that the industry be able to survive in the end without any protection whatsoever. Otherwise, losses go on ad infinitum. Consequently, at the same time a decision is made to subsidize an infant industry, a choice of the time when such protection is to be phased out should be made simultaneously. Such industries have a pernicious tendency to not want to be weaned from the public trough.

THE EFFECTIVE RATE OF PROTECTION

When the production of a good requires intermediate inputs that have tariff rates different from the final good, it is necessary to adjust the nominal rate of protection indicated by the tariff rate, τ, on the final good to find the effective rate of protection, e, provided by the entire tariff structure, which includes the tariff rates on intermediate inputs, t_i. In general, the tariff rates on final goods are greater than those levied on intermediate inputs, so that as a result the effective rate of protection to domestic value added is greater than the tariff rate on final goods. This phenomenon is called *tariff cascading* and is widely felt to discourage higher stages of processing in developing countries since it affords

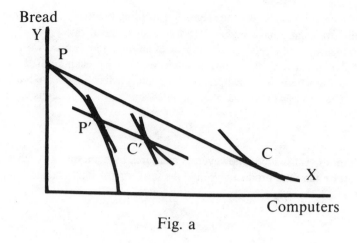

Fig. a

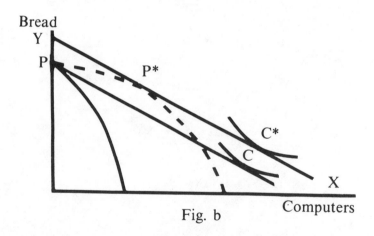

Fig. b

FIGURE 6-6. The Infant Industry Argument for Protection. Short-term, temporary losses are sustained from tariff protection to the computer industry. Protection permits production at point P' in Figure 6-6a, but taxes consumption at point C'. Following a period of technological progress, which shifts the production frontier outward in Figure 6-6b, the country can compete at the world price, producing at P^* and consuming at C^*. If further protection had been necessary, this investment in an infant industry would not have been worthwhile.

greater protection the higher the stage of processing involved. Developing countries also frequently have higher effective than nominal rates.

To measure the effective rate of protection on a good whose world price is P and that uses a_i units of intermediate input i for each unit of the good produced and where the world prices of the intermediate inputs are indicated by p_i, it is first necessary to note that value added at world prices is given by

$$v = P - \Sigma a_i p_i.$$

Domestic value added, however, is measured by domestic prices that include the tariff on the final product, τP, and the tariff on the intermediate inputs, $t_i p_i$, or

$$v' = P\,(1+\tau) - \Sigma a_i p_i\,(1+t_i).$$

Consequently, we may define the effective rate of protection to domestic value added as $e = (v' - v)/v$, or

$$e = \frac{[P\,(1+\tau) - \Sigma a_i p_i\,(1+t_i)] - [P - \Sigma a_i p_i]}{v}$$

$$= \frac{(P - \Sigma a_i p_i) + (P\tau - \Sigma a_i p_i t_i) - (P - \Sigma a_i p_i)}{v}$$

$$= \frac{P\tau - \Sigma a_i p_i t_i}{v}$$

$$= \frac{P\tau - \Sigma a_i p_i \tau + \Sigma a_i p_i \tau - \Sigma a_i p_i t_i}{v}$$

$$= \frac{(P - \Sigma a_i p_i)\tau + \Sigma(\tau - t_i)a_i p_i}{v}$$

$$= \tau + \frac{\Sigma(\tau - t_i)a_i p_i}{v}.$$

Consequently, if the tariff rate on the final good exceeds the tariff rates on intermediate inputs—or $\tau > t_i$, for all i—the effective rate of protection exceeds the nominal rate of protection. In general, tariff rates on some of the inputs may be less than the rate on the final good and yet effective protection be greater than nominal protection, provided that a weighted average of input tariffs is greater than the nominal tariff on the final good. To ensure that there is no discrepancy between effective and nominal rates of protection, Arnold Harberger (1984) has argued in favor of uniform tariff rates on all goods. Finally, it should be pointed out that when no intermediate inputs are used, or $a=0$, the effective rate of protection equals the nominal rate, or $e=\tau$.

CONCLUSION

While it is clear that any tariff or trade restriction tends to cause a loss in world welfare, a specific country or group of countries may gain by imposing a trade restriction to turn the terms of trade in their favor. This is the so-called optimum tariff argument, which requires a tariff equal to the reciprocal of the foreign elasticity of supply. Foreign retaliation may leave the tariff-initiating country worse off, however. In addition, any tariff can be duplicated by an identical tax on exports since it is trade that is taxed, not imports. This is the famous Lerner symmetry theorem.

Other arguments for tariffs include the infant industry argument and the domestic unemployment argument. While both are seen to have some merit under certain circumstances, a direct production subsidy to the infant industry or the import-competing industry in distress is a superior policy to protection by a tariff since it does not unnecessarily tax the consumer. Finally, when tariff rates on imported inputs are lower than tariff rates on final goods, the effective rate of protection enjoyed by final goods is greater than the nominal rate. Typically, this is the case.

SELECTED READINGS

Baldwin, Robert. 1948. "Equilibrium in International Trade: A Diagrammatic Analysis." *Quarterly Journal of Economics* (November).

Ethier, Wilfred J. 1977. "The Theory of Effective Protection in General Equilibrium: Effective-Rate Analogues of Nominal Rates." *Canadian Journal of Economics* (May).

Graaff, J. de V. 1949. "On Optimum Tariff Structures." *Review of Economic Studies*.

Harberger, Arnold. 1984. "Economic Policy and Economic Growth." In *World Economic Growth*, edited by A. Harberger. San Francisco: ICS Press.

Johnson, Harry. 1953/54. "Optimum Tariffs and Retaliation." *Review of Economic Studies*.

Krueger, Anne. 1966. "Some Economic Costs of Exchange Control: The Turkish Case." *Journal of Political Economy* (October).

Lerner, Abba. 1936. "Symmetry between Import and Export Taxes." *Economica* (August).

McKinnon, Ronald. 1966. "Intermediate Products, Differential Tariffs, and a Generalization of Lerner's Symmetry Theorem." *Quarterly Journal of Economics* (November).

Melvin, James. 1970. "Commodity Taxes as a Determinant of Trade." *Canadian Journal of Economics* 3 (February).

Metzler, L. A. 1949. "Tariffs, the Terms of Trade, and the Distribution of National Income." *Journal of Political Economy* (February).

Scitovsky, Tibor. 1942. "A Re-Consideration of the Theory of Tariffs." *Review of Economic Studies* 9 (Summer). Reprinted in the AEA *Readings in the Theory of International Trade,* edited by H. S. Ellis and L. S. Metzler. Homewood, Illinois: R. D. Irwin Co, 1950.

SEVEN

FOREIGN LENDING

The international debt crisis of the 1980s has underlined the importance of foreign lending in the international economic system. Lending is truly international these days. In a simple sense, lending is trade in income over time where the interest rate plays the role of the intertemporal terms of trade. In large part the international debt crisis is the result of a massive worsening of the terms of trade of developing countries through a decline in the relative price of primary commodities, a rise then a fall in the relative price of oil, and a rise in the real rate of interest. Adjustment to these shocks via the running of large budget and trade deficits has exhausted foreign reserves, leaving debtor nations in many instances unable to service their foreign debt. The pursuit of monetary policies more expansionary than warranted by rates of exchange rate depreciation in order to finance these deficits led in addition to speculative attacks on central bank reserves, making debt repayment all the more difficult. This chapter focuses on foreign lending as trade over time, thus bringing the apparatus of trade theory to bear on problems of international indebtedness.

CORRESPONDENCE WITH TRADE THEORY

Borrowing and lending are processes involving time. A lender can always be said to sacrifice the present in return for future reward, whereas a borrower draws upon the future to live (consume or invest) beyond his or her current means. In other words a borrower is one who supplies future income; a lender is one who demands it. In terms of present income a lender is a supplier, and a borrower is a demander. In terms of securities, or present contracts for future income, the roles are reversed: a lender is a demander and a borrower is a supplier. Further, for any individual (or country) the supply of loans equals, in value, the demand for repayments, and the value of the debts incurred equals the value of future repayments. This is, in fact, Mill's law of reciprocal demand applied to trade over time. To press the analogy of lending with trade over time, we can treat a lender much like an exporter: exports consist of present income, and imports are made up of claims to future income. A borrower, on the other hand, imports present income and exports current indebtedness. Interest rates play the role of terms of trade over time, and equilibrium entails finding those terms of trade that equate desired exports and imports. In familiar terms, rates of interest serve to equate desired loans and borrowings.

In what follows we outline a theory of international capital movements that parallels the theory of international trade by treating lending as trade over time, an approach that can be traced directly to the work of Irving Fisher (1954). As with Fisher, the "supply and demand we have to deal with are . . . the supply and demand of future income" (p. 32), and we will treat an interest rate as "that sort of price which links one point of time with another point of time in the markets of the world" (p. 33). From a strictly Fisherian point of view, capital theory involves exchange over time and is therefore simply another dimension of trade theory. Whereas the latter typically restricts exchange to the same point in time, there is no reason to do so. Present goods can exchange for present goods, but they can also exchange for future goods through borrowing and lending. It is one and the same thing: an exchange of commodities. Whether it is an exchange of home for foreign goods at the same point of time or over time makes little difference. Nor does it matter that the price of present goods in terms of future goods is expressed in terms of a percentage premium called the *interest rate*—we are still dealing with terms of trade over time.

THE INVESTMENT OPPORTUNITY SCHEDULE

Identifying with America, let us first explore the savings and investment opportunities open to a country in the absence of borrowing from abroad. To be more concrete, we will first develop an investment opportunity schedule indicating the fashion in which America can best transform present income into future income through the process of investment. We will consider only one commodity, wine, which can be consumed now or carried over to the future for consumption then. By virtue of the assumption of two time periods, the present and the future, we have from an economic point of view two goods: present wine and future wine. To further simplify matters, we will suppose that in the initial time period America begins with an initial output of wine that is determined by the resource base of the economy combined with the state of the techniques for converting them into the final product, wine. The maximum amount of production of wine is thus the initial quantity available in the present period and can be put to two uses—either consumption or investment. A bottle of wine can be drunk now, or it can be stored in the cellar till next year when it can be consumed then. This laying away for the future is the type of investment we have in mind. The total value of investment equals, of course, the value of production less the value of consumption. It is a matter of definition, and while it corresponds exactly to that used in the national income accounts, we are merely saying here that if there are 500 bottles available now, and 400 of them are drunk in the present, there will be 100 carried over to the future.

We are also interested, however, in the corresponding amounts of wine that can be consumed in the future. If production conditions do not vary from the present to the future, America could presumably produce the same amount as before, the 500 bottles, plus consume the 100 bottles previously laid aside. If wine carried over from the first sitting neither mellowed nor soured with age, the corresponding consumption possibility available in the future would be 600 bottles of comparable quality. What we are describing here is a way in which present wine is translated into future wine; and by assumption we take initially a case in which, from the investment side, the wine stored over a lapse of time is indistinguishable form newly produced wine. There is neither an improvement in nor a worsening of quality. If we put this possibility in terms of rates of return to investment, the rate of return to wine, expressed in terms of wine, is zero. Equivalently, a bottle of present wine can be transformed into a bottle of future wine, neither more nor less. The aging process does not improve it, for then the rate of return to investment would be positive; nor does it injure the quality, for then the rate of return would be negative.

In short, were we to express this relationship graphically, the consumption pattern available to America over time would consist of: (1) in the present, the current level of production less investment and (2) in the future, the future level of production plus previous investment. The rate of return to investment is zero—or one unit of current investment gives rise to exactly one unit of future consumption. Another way of looking at the problem is that the production frontier between present and future wine is linear, with a slope or opportunity cost equal to unity. This situation is shown in Figure 7-1. The productive capacity of America is indicated by the length of OP along the horizontal axis, whereas its future productive capacity is indicated by the length of OP' along the vertical axis. Since we assume no change in the underlying resource and technical base of the economy from the present to the future, the productive capacities are the same now and in the future, or $OP=OP'$; the corresponding production pattern C' is therefore equidistant from both axes.

The point C' is also one consumption possibility available to America and would involve consuming the full amount of wine capable of being produced in the same period in which it is made available. In the absence of borrowing from abroad, America could not consume more wine in the present than OP, the amount produced. The economy may, however, consume less now for the purpose of consuming tomorrow even more than the quantity produced in the fu-

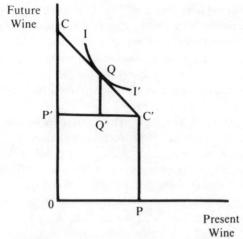

FIGURE 7-1. America: Present and Future. The productive capacity of America remains unchanged in the future, so that the equal segments OP and OP' summarize the levels of present and future wine production. American wine, neither improving nor worsening with age, is set aside for future consumption, one bottle sacrificed today giving rise to one bottle tomorrow, as indicated by the slope of minus unity of CC'. The optimum consumption pattern over time is at Q; investment equals $C'Q'$ bottles, or the total value of current production, $P'C'$, less current consumption, $P'Q'$. As in the Ricardian trade model with constant opportunity costs, prices (or interest rates, in this context) are determined solely by production conditions. In the special case illustrated, the rate of return to investment is zero, independent of the level of investment.

ture. This possibility is entirely open to the economy taken collectively, for it means simply that on the average individuals are setting aside wine to be consumed tomorrow. Further, since the wine neither improves nor worsens, a bottle of wine invested today matures into one bottle tomorrow. The consumption possibility curve implied by this is the straight line CC', having a slope equal to -1. Consuming one additional bottle of wine today rather than putting it aside for investment has an opportunity cost of one bottle of future wine sacrificed. To take into account the demand side, we sketch in the highest indifference curve, II', attainable for society, tangent to the consumption possibility curve CC' at point Q. This indifference curve represents the combinations of present and future consumption that leave America indifferent to consumption at point Q. Its slope is, as usual, the marginal rate of substitution between present and future income, just as the slope of CC' is the opportunity cost of present in terms of future income. The optimal time pattern of consumption requires that these rates be equal, a requirement that is by now a quite familiar one.

It is customary, however, to call these curves and their slopes by another name because we are dealing with time. The production frontier, for instance, is called the *investment opportunity schedule*. It indicates the amount by which future consumption can be increased for each level of investment undertaken in the present. At Q the level of investment is $Q'C'$ — or equivalently, the present production of wine less that quantity consumed—and the corresponding reward in future wine is QQ'. The slope of the investment opportunity schedule, $QQ'/Q'C'$, is used to define the rate of return to investment, the increase in future income as a percentage of present investment, or

$$g = \frac{QQ' - Q'C'}{Q'C'}$$

$$= \frac{QQ'}{Q'C'} - 1$$

$$= \text{Absolute value of slope } CC' - 1,$$

where g is defined as the rate of return to investment.

THE TIME PREFERENCE SCHEDULE

In Figure 7-1 one unit of present wine carries over into one unit of future wine, so $QQ' = Q'C'$, and the corresponding rate of return to investment is zero. A more steeply sloped investment schedule would mean a positive rate of return, and a flatter one would indicate a negative rate of return. The indifference curve is called a *time preference schedule*, and its slope is used to define the *marginal rate of time preference*. If it exceeds 1, in absolute value, there is said to be a positive time preference, whereas if it falls short of 1, there exists negative time preference. In the first case more than one unit of future income is required to compensate for a unit sacrificed in present income, whereas in the second case less than one unit is required. It is a way of defining, for any particular consumption pattern, the direction of bias in present and future consumption preferences.

We are using the term marginal rate of time preference in its general form to refer to the slope of the time preference schedule at any particular pattern of consumption over time, not only at equal levels of consumption. The interesting thing is that no matter what the preference pattern, provided that some investment takes place, there will be zero time preference. Putting it in another way, since the marginal rate of time preference is defined as $1 + r$, the rate of discount, r, on future consumption must equal zero, no matter what the preference pattern is (assuming some investment, of course).

This result is strikingly similar to the Ricardian case of constant opportunity costs in which demand conditions do not play a role in determining price. In fact the result is identical. In the time preference framework, for price to be determined by production means that the rate of interest is determined solely by the rate of return to investment, g, a constant, and not at all by preferences. As in the Ricardian framework, comparative advantage in present over future income would be determined by the slopes of the respective investment opportunity schedules. As long as they differ, exchange over time will take place.

EQUILIBRIUM INTEREST RATE: CLOSED ECONOMY

However, there is no reason to restrict ourselves to the case of constant opportunity costs. We can easily allow for diminishing rates of return to investment or—what is the same thing—increasing opportunity costs of transforming present into future income. This gets us away from a purely mechanical way of determining rates of interest. It is no longer possible to find an equilibrium interest rate by knowing the investment schedules in two countries. The conditions of supply no longer suffice since demand comes into play. In the absence of trade the interest rate in each country is thus determined in a very familiar manner: It is that rate that brings into equality the rate of return to investment, g, and the rate of time preference, r, at the margin, where both rates vary according to the amount of investment.

In Figure 7–2 the investment opportunity schedule, PP', is concave everywhere, reflecting the assumption of a diminishing marginal rate of return to investment: the more wine put away in the present, the smaller the return in terms of future wine—even when done efficiently. The time preference schedule, II', is convex everywhere, reflecting an increasing marginal rate of time preference; the more wine foregone in the present, the greater the amount of future wine necessary to compensate for the increased sacrifice. The slope of PP' is $-(1+g)$, whereas that of II' is $-(1+r)$; and at the point of tangency, Q, one finds the equilibrium interest rate for the closed economy.

All rates are equal at the equilibrium position: the marginal rate of return on investment and the interest rate for the economy. In short, we have a situation that completely parallels the determination of the relative price of two goods at the same point in time by the tangency of the production frontier and the indifference map. As Fisher (1954) describes it, in his subtitle to *The Theory of Interest*, the equilibrium interest rate is determined by "IMPATIENCE To Spend Income and OPPORTUNITY To Invest It" (p.v.).

Similarly, in the absence of foreign lending, the interest rate in Europe is determined by the conjunction of supply and demand conditions. Europe also is willing to trade various amounts of income over time, depending upon the rate of interest realized. Let us suppose that Europe's prelending interest rate is lower than America's, so that America borrows from Europe. At the risk of being

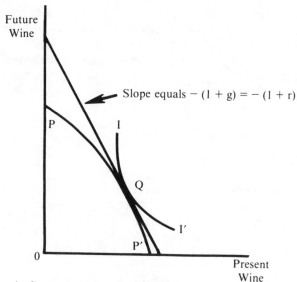

Slope equals $- (1 + g) = - (1 + r)$

FIGURE 7–2. Equilibrium Interest Rate: Closed Economy. The graph brings together the investment opportunity schedule and the time preference schedules, thereby determining, at Q, their tangency, the rate at which present wine is exchanged for future wine. In Fisher's inimitable terms, the equilibrium interest rate is determined by "IMPATIENCE To Spend Income and OPPORTUNITY To Invest It" (Fisher 1954, p. v.).

repetitive, the equilibrium interest rate must lie between those that would reign in the absence of foreign lending, and it must be a rate that brings into equality the amount of present income that Europe is willing to lend with the amount that America desires to borrow. In both countries the amounts of income borrowed and lent depend upon the terms of trade over time—for example, $1 + r$, which gives the number of units of future income to be paid in exchange for one unit of present income.

EQUILIBRIUM WITH LENDING ABROAD

If we now allow for the opportunity of borrowing or lending abroad, America will borrow or import present income at lower rates of interest, whereas it will lend or export present income at higher rates of interest. Further, America will potentially gain from this exchange of income over time. Indeed, one can easily derive a foreign indebtedness schedule conceptually identical to the trade offer curve by facing America with various foreign interest rates and finding the amounts it is willing to borrow or lend. By varying the rate of exchange, the reciprocal demand curves are found, and their intersection determines the equilibrium interest rate. As drawn in Figure 7-3, interest rates in both countries are positive before trade. That is, the slopes of the offer curves both exceed unity at the origin. After trade, the interest rate in Europe, the lending country, is greater, whereas it is lower in America, the borrower. Barring impediments, foreign lending brings into equality the rates of return to investment, the rates of time preference, and the rates of interest.

CONCLUSION

International lending can be treated as trade in income over time where, in Fisher's (1954) terms, "the supply and demand we have to deal with are ... the supply and demand of future income" and the interest rate—"that sort of price which links one point of time with another point of time in the markets of the world" (pp. 32–33). In the absence of foreign lending the domestic rate

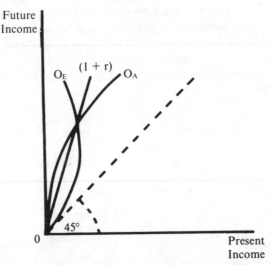

FIGURE 7-3. America Borrows From Europe. In the absence of foreign borrowing or lending, the equilibrium price of present income in terms of future income in America and Europe equal, respectively, the slopes of the offer curves at the origin 0. As drawn, both interest rates are positive (the slopes at the origin exceed unity), but America borrows from Europe since the interest rate there is lower. In the terminology of trade theory, America has a comparative advantage in future income, whereas Europe has a comparative advantage in present income. Borrowing from abroad has the effect of equalizing world interest rates and rates of return.

of interest will be determined by the investment opportunity schedule and the marginal rate of time preference in the same manner that relative prices are determined by the production frontier and the indifference schedule. When foreign lending is possible, the country with the previously lower rate of interest will have a comparative advantage in current income and will thus lend abroad, whereas the country with a higher rate of interest will have a comparative advantage in future income and will consequently borrow abroad. International borrowing and lending leads to gains in welfare in the sense that more goods are potentially available in all periods to all individuals. That is, there are gains to trade over time. When desired loans and borrowings are equal, the equilibrium rate of interest is established worldwide.

SELECTED READINGS

Armella, Pedro Aspe, Rudiger Dornbusch, and Maurice Obstfeld, 1983. *Financial Policies and the World Capital Market: The Problem of Latin American Countries*. Chicago: University of Chicago Press.

Baldwin, Robert. 1966. "The Role of Capital Goods Trade in the Theory of International Trade." *American Economic Review* (September).

Claassen, Emil-Maria. 1985. "The Latin American Debt Problem and the Lender-of-Last Resort Function." In *The Economics of the Caribbean Basin*, edited by Michael Connolly and John McDermott. New York: Praeger.

Connolly, Michael, and Stephen Ross. 1970. "A Fisherian Approach to Trade, Capital Movements, and Tariffs." *American Economic Review* (June).

Fisher, Irving. 1954. *The Theory of Interest as Determined by IMPATIENCE To Spend Income and OPPORTUNITY To Invest It*. New York: Kelley & Millman, Inc.

Leontief, Wassily. 1958. "Theoretical Note on Time-Preference, Productivity of Capital, Stagnation, and Economic Growth." *American Economic Review* (March).

Melvin, James. 1970. "A General Equilibrium Theory of International Capital Flows: A Comment." *Economic Journal* (September).

Miller, Norman. 1968. "A General Equilibrium Theory of International Capital Flows." *Economic Journal* (June).

Sjaastad, Larry. 1983. "The International Debt Quagmire: To Whom Do We Owe It?" *World Economy* (September).

EIGHT

TAXES ON TRADE AND LENDING

This chapter integrates trade in commodities at the same point in time and over time. Integration allows for a simultaneous treatment of taxes related to international trade and taxes affecting foreign lending. We focus specifically on (1) the optimum tariff on commodities and (2) tax on capital movements, which seek the optimum nationalistic improvement in the terms of trade. In this context the *terms of trade* refer not only to the relative price of export goods but also to the interest rate at which the home country borrows or lends. Once again, this type of nationalistic commerical and capital policy is clearly not optimal from a worldwide point of view.

The element of time plays a major role. It allows for a current account deficit financed by an equal and opposite capital account surplus. This defines equilibrium in the balance of payments and means that if a country is a net importer of goods in the present, it simultaneously incurs debt of the same value. This debt, in turn, can be thought of as an export of claims to future commodity repayments. Equilibrium entails that the present value of its future exports equals the value of its current imports.

In short, in this framework it is not necessary that current exports pay for current imports. A country borrows when the value of its current exports falls short of the value of its current imports, the difference being the exact value of its new debt.

We can now raise the question of optimal taxes on exchange, choosing the term *exchange* to represent both taxes on trade in current goods and trade in contacts for future goods. Once again, a country stands to gain in taxing exchange over time in the same manner as it may in taxing exchange at the same point of time. It has the same purpose: to influence the terms of trade. That the terms of trade over time are called interest rates or that a lender is treated as an exporter and a borrower an importer of present income makes little difference. The optimum tax on borrowing from abroad, like the optimum tariff, is simply the reciprocal of the foreign elasticity of loans with respect to the intertemporal terms of trade. For America the optimum tax on borrowing has the purpose of bringing into equality the marginal cost of borrowing funds from Europe with the domestic marginal rates of return to investment and time preference. The problem, of course, is that additional borrowing from Europe tends to bid up the interest rate paid and that this monopoly power collective to the community is to be taken into account.

How might we express the argument in terms of interest rates? Recall that loans from Europe to America, Z, are equal to the amount of savings done by Europeans, S, less the amount they invest at home, I. Note further that both savings and investment in Europe depend upon the level of the interest rate, r. We have, then, $Z=S-I$, and $\epsilon_{zp}=(S/Z)\epsilon_{sp}+(I/Z)\epsilon_{ip}$, where $p=1+r$. That is, the foreign elasticity of supply of loans with respect to the intertemporal terms of trade equals a weighted sum of the foreign elasticity of savings and investment schedules. This is no more than the formula previously derived for the optimum tariff, where the elasticity of the supply of exports equals a weighted sum of the foreign elasticities of supply and demand (see Chapter 6). But how are terms of trade elasticities related to interest rate elasticities? Clearly, since $p=1+r$, a change in the rate of interest entails an equal change in the intertemporal terms of trade. It follows that the change in the supply of loans must be the same, or $\dfrac{\partial Z}{\partial r}=\dfrac{\partial Z}{\partial p}$. In terms of percentage changes, or elasticities, however, we have

$\epsilon_{zp}=\dfrac{p}{z}\ \dfrac{\partial z}{\partial p}=[(1+r)/r][r/z]\dfrac{\partial z}{\partial r}=[(1+r)/r]\ \epsilon_{zr}$. Verbally, the elasticity of supply of loans with respect to the terms of trade equals the ratio $(1+r)/r$ times the elasticity with respect to the interest rate. For example, if the terms of trade elasticity were 2 at a 10 percent interest rate, the corresponding interest elasticity would be 2/11, or slightly less than 20 percent. This relationship holds for all elasticities; in one case the percentage change in price is measured; in the other it is the percentage change in the premium. In short, $\epsilon_{sp}=[(1+r)/r]\epsilon_{sr}$ and $\epsilon_{ip}=[(1+r)/r]\epsilon_{ir}$. Finally, let us define one last measure, $\mu=Z/I$, the amount Europeans invest in America expressed as a percentage of their domestic investment. Bringing these various measures together, and noting that the optimal tax on loans from abroad is the reciprocal of the foreign elasticity of supply with respect to the terms of trade, the optimal tax on borrowing is given by (from Connolly and Ross [1970]):

$$\tau=\dfrac{1}{\dfrac{(1+r)}{r}\ [(1+1/\mu)\ \epsilon_{sr}+(1/\mu)\ \epsilon_{ir}]}\ . \qquad 8.1$$

The optimum tax formula lends itself easily to interpretation. Holding other variables in the formula constant:

1. The greater μ loans made by Europe to America as a percent of their domestic investment, the larger the optimal tax on borrowing;
2. The greater the foreign savings and investment elasticities, the smaller the optimal tax on borrowings; and
3. The higher the interest rate, the greater the optimal tax.

As an illustrative exercise, we can substitute some hypothetical figures into the optimal tax formula. Suppose, for example, that interest rates are 10 percent and that the price elasticities of European savings and investment equal unity, so that their interest elasticities are 1/11. Also, let borrowings be 1/6 of what Europeans invest at home. In this instance the optimal tax levied by America would be 1/13, or about 8 percent of the loan. If Europe's loans were only 1/12 of its investment at home, and the other variables were the same, the optimum tax rate would fall to 1/25, or 4 percent, reflecting America's small size in Europe's capital market.

OPTIMUM TAX ON FOREIGN LENDING

As a lender, Europe can also play the game of optimum taxes. Their purpose is to restrict the amount lent abroad in order to receive an optimal return at the margin. The argument is perfectly symmetrical, so that if we let μ^* equal $-\mu$, the ratio of Europe's loans to total investment by Americans, the optimal tax on foreign lending is

$$\tau' = \frac{1}{\left(\dfrac{1+r}{r} \right) \left[\left(\dfrac{1}{\mu^*} \right) \epsilon_{ir} + \left(\dfrac{1}{\mu^*} - 1 \right) \epsilon_{sr} \right] - 1} \, , \qquad 8.2$$

where the term in the denominator is America's demand-elasticity for loans minus unity. Once again, the optimum tax on lending abroad varies inversely with the foreign savings and investment elasticities and positively with respect to interest rates and the relative size of Europe in America's capital market. In short, as in tariff theory, the optimum tax structure depends upon the monopoly power of the home country in world capital markets.

In Chapter 6 we discussed the consequences of a sequence of retaliation in the context of optimum tariff theory. Recall that the strategy adopted by both countries involves the imposition of an optimum tax on the Cournot assumption that the foreign country will not retaliate. If the tax reaction curve process comes to a stable halt, either both countries are worse off or one benefits—but only at the expense of the other. Further, in the latter case it is not necessarily the country that taxes first that gains.

QUANTITATIVE CONTROLS ON CAPTIAL MOVEMENTS

In many instances the impediment imposed on foreign lending takes the form of a quantitative restriction, either of a binding or a voluntary nature. This is particularly true in times of crisis and capital flight, but it frequently becomes, or is a deliberate part of, a fairly lengthy balance of payments policy. A natural question arises: How can quantitative restrictions on capital movements be analyzed and what gains and losses are made and by whom? The first part of the question is readily handled: a quantitative control on foreign lending can be treated in the same manner as a quota on current trade. By curbing the supply of loans abroad, foreign rates of return tend to rise, whereas domestic rates fall, just as an export quota causes the foreign price to rise and the domestic price to fall. Who gains and who loses? The standard answer is that differences in the rates of return entail investment inefficiency, and the world as a whole tends to lose owing to the partial reversal of the gains to unfettered free trade and foreign investment. In general, some gain while others lose (more, if compared to the free trade situation). Those firms and banks that elude, or are exempted from, the controls tend to realize greater returns from their foreign investment but lower returns on domestic investments. Similarly, lenders abroad receive higher rates of interest, whereas borrowers suffer from the rise. At home the opposite is true: borrowers gain, while lenders lose. Further, as with a quota, the premium on foreign loans gives rise to a sort of revenue profit to the export of capital that can—in theory—be captured by or distributed among (1) the restricting government, by an appropriate tax or license policy; (2) those domestic firms, banks, and investors that lend abroad at a higher interest rate; or (3) those borrowers abroad, whether of domestic or foreign origin, that benefit if the rate charged on foreign loans is not increased while other rates abroad rise.

Further, if trade is to balance, and foreign lending is curbed, repercussions on the current account are to be expected. We will now consider trade in current goods to analyze repercussions on the current account. To do so, we must deal with at least four commodities, for example, trade in bread and wine not only in the present and the future but also between the present and the future. Note that we stress the point that the same physical items, bread and wine, available at different points in time must be considered as different commodities. So once again we accent the theme of foreign lending as trade over time. While the analysis necessitates a higher level of difficulty, the familiar optimum tariff argument is applied to exchange over time. Consequently, it becomes clear that one need not treat taxes on capital movements as a species different than taxes on trade in goods. It is trade that is taxed, and the purpose is the same—to influence the terms on which it takes place. That the terms of trade over time are called interest rates makes no difference. From this point of view the optimum tax-tariff structure entails the familiar equalization of the domestic and foreign marginal rates of transformation through trade and foreign lending.

CURRENT AND CAPITAL ACCOUNTS

To simplify matters, again let us eliminate the problem of uncertainty. Present and future production and consumption possibilities are assumed to be perfectly known today, and all economic actors—importers, exporters, borrowers, and lenders—take prices as given. Current markets exist in which contracts for delivery in the future are made. Today's prices for future delivery correctly reflect future relative scarcities since everyone enjoys perfect information.

With perfect future markets, individuals make contracts payable in the present for delivery in both periods. Identifying once more with America, let us represent foreign prices in the following way:

	Bread	*Wine*
Present	P_1^0	P_1^0
Future	P_1^1	P_2^1

Superscripts 0 and 1 refer to prices charged today for present and future delivery, whereas subscripts 1 and 2 denote bread and wine, respectively. Since only relative prices count, the above are in terms of some abstract unit of account, say bancors, that play no role; only their ratios matter. For instance, P_1^0/P_2^0 is the rate at which bread and wine can be traded in the present; and P_1^1/P_2^1 is the rate at which future bread and wine are exchanged. Note that since we assume perfect foresight, there can be no divergence between the present price of bread in terms of wine for future delivery and the relative price that prevails in the future period. All contracts are made now, and they are met without fault. The prices of contracts for future delivery, P_1^1 and P_2^1, can be thought of as the present value in bancors of one unit of the good promised for future delivery. The premium on present bread in terms of future bread, $(P_1^0-P_1^1)/P_1^1$, defines the bread rate of interest, and $(P_2^0-P_1^1)/P_1^1$ defines the wine rate of interest. It will become clear that they are not necessarily equal. For the moment, however, we are only interested in the corresponding terms of trade over time, P_1^0/P_1^1 and P_2^0/P_2^1.

America's imports of each commodity can be represented similarly by the same notation:

	Bread	Wine
Present	Z_1^0	Z_2^0
Future	Z_1^1	Z_2^1

A positive value indicates net imports, whereas a negative value represents exports. For exports, American consumption exceeds production, whereas for imports, production exceeds consumption. The trade possibilities are numerous: America could import both wine and bread in the present and export both in the future, which would represent a clear case of borrowing today with repayment tomorrow. By the same token, negative values of Z_1^0 and Z_2^0, indicating exports of both commodities in the present, combined with positive values of Z_1^1 and Z_2^1, indicating future imports, would represent a clear case of lending. There are less obvious cases, however. Suppose America imports wine in the present but exports it in the future while at the same time is exporting bread in the present and importing it in the future. Can America be said to borrow wine and lend bread? Not in a meaningful sense, because borrowing and lending cannot in general be identified with trade in a particular commodity. In particular a country may well export machinery and equipment, but this does not necessarily imply that it is lending abroad. If the value of its exports falls short of the value of imports, the country is incurring debt rather than lending. What constitutes borrowing or lending over time depends upon whether or not imports pay for exports in the present; so this is purely a net concept. If imports and exports just cancel, the country is neither borrowing nor lending.

On the one hand, if a country is borrowing, it simultaneously must offer claims on future goods equal to the value of its debt, whereas if it is lending, it demands such claims. In other words, while the terms Z_1^1 and Z_2^1 equal future imports of each commodity, they also represent purchases of securities by the home country in the present. Each security entitles the holder to the future import of one unit of the commodity in which it is denominated. Clearly, then, the net value of imports in the present must be just matched by the net value of exports of such claims. In short, if there is a trade deficit on current account there must be an equal and opposite surplus on capital account (equation 8.3). The balance of payments is thus in equilibrium when

$$F = P_1^0 Z_1^0 + P_2^0 Z_2^0 + P_1^1 Z_1^1 + P_2^1 Z_2^1 = 0. \qquad (8.3)$$

The equation expresses the relationship that the present value of the balance of trade must be zero. Or, it states that the balance on current account must exactly cancel the balance on capital account.

Following J. de V. Graaff (1949), we will call F the *foreign trade transformation function* facing America. If we assume that each price is a differentiable function of all imports, F can be differentiated with respect to each import item to derive the marginal rates of transformation through foreign trade facing the home country:

$$-\frac{dZ_j^\tau}{dZ_i^t} = \frac{\partial F}{\partial Z_i^t} \Big/ \frac{\partial F}{\partial Z_j^\tau} = \frac{P_i^t(1+a_i^t)}{P_j^\tau(1+a_j^\tau)} \; ;$$

where

$$t,\tau=0,\ 1$$
$$i,j=1,\ 2 \tag{8.4}$$

$$a_i^t \equiv \sum_{(\alpha,k)} \frac{\partial P_k^\alpha}{\partial Z_i^t} \frac{Z_k^\alpha}{P_i^t} \; .$$

It is convenient to express the a_i^t terms in the following way:

$$a_i^t = \sum_{(\alpha,k)} \eta_{it}^{k\alpha} \frac{P_k^\alpha Z_k^\alpha}{P_i^t Z_i^t} \; ;$$

$$i,\ k=1,\ 2$$
$$t,\ \alpha=0,\ 1\ . \tag{8.5}$$

where $\eta_{it}^{k\alpha}$ is the percentage change in the price P_k^α divided by the percentage change in extra imports of Z_i^t. It is thus an elasticity that gives a measure of the relative impact on the price of each traded good and claim as a result of extra imports of the i'th good in period t. The remaining terms serve as weights: they give the value of trade in each and every item relative to trade in the i'th good at point t in time. Their purpose is to distinguish the degree of importance to be attached to the change in the price of each item. The a_i^t terms in equation 8.4 are thus the sums of the foreign quantity elasticities, each weighted by the ratio of the value of trade in that good to the value of trade in Z_i^t. They express the marginal cost to the home country of changes in the terms of trade induced by additional imports of i in period t. Consequently, $P_i^t(1+a_i^t)$ is the total marginal cost in the present to the home country of increasing such imports—or analogously, the present marginal export revenue if Z_i^t is negative. If the home country can have no effect whatsoever on any price, all the a_i^t terms are zero. From equation 8.4 this absence of monopoly power means that the marginal rates of transformation through trade equal the foreign relative prices.

OPTIMUM TAXES ON EXCHANGE

In the absence of externalities, Pareto optimality requires the equality of the domestic marginal rates of substitution in consumption (DRS) and the domestic marginal rates of transformation (DRT). In an open economy both must be brought into equality with the marginal rates of transformation through foreign trade. These conditions are unaltered when exchange over time is included along with exchange at a given moment of time. On the assumption that the domestic price ratio π_i^t/π_j^t reflects the DRS and the DRT, the efficiency conditions become

$$\frac{\pi_i^t}{\pi_i^\tau} = \frac{P_i^t(1+a_i^t)}{P_i^\tau(1+a_j^\tau)} \; ; \quad \begin{matrix} t,\tau=0,1 \\ i,j=1,2 \end{matrix} . \tag{8.6}$$

Pareto optimality may then be satisfied by levying an ad valorem tax equal algebraically to a_i^t on each good i traded at time t. For commodities traded in the present, the tax is expressed as a percentage of the foreign commodity price. For trade in contracts to future commodities, the tax is expressed as a percentage of the current foreign price of the claim entitling the holder to future delivery of one unit of the commodity in which it is denominated. We have, in short, taxes levied simultaneously on goods and securities in the present. The taxes are payable in the present and not necessarily when the good crosses the border. If the taxes were payable upon delivery, they would be costed up at an appropriate interest rate.

In our example this procedure defines a system of four tariffs, some of which may be subsidies owing to cross effects. This happens when the own effects are outweighed by substitutability and complementarity effects. For instance, it might be worthwhile to subsidize exports of wine in the present if this makes for cheaper wine imports in the future. From equation 8.5 this situation is most likely to arise if the value of present wine exports is small relative to the value of future wine exports.

In summary it should be clear that the formulas and the results of this section generalize simply to the case of an arbitrary number of goods, time periods, and countries.

INTEREST RATES

In principle the task of finding optimum taxes on trade and lending is finished. We need not take up the problem of interest rates since the equivalent information is given by the terms of trade over time. To aid in the interpretation of the above formulas, however, it is worthwhile to translate some of the relationships into the language of interest rates. In particular let us take a look at the relationship that interest rates bear, first, to foreign interest rates and, second, to one another. We have two standards in which interest rates can be expressed: in bread and in wine. Letting r_1 and r_1^* denote the foreign and domestic rates of interest in terms of bread, the relationship between the own interest rates is, as before, $P_1^0/P_1^1 = 1+r$ and $(P_1^0/P_1^1)^* = 1+r_1^*$. Thus, from equation 8.6 we have

$$\frac{1+r_i^*}{1+r_i} = \frac{1+a_i^0}{1+a_i^1}; \quad i=1,2. \tag{8.7}$$

It follows that the domestic rate of interest in good i exceeds the foreign one if, and only if, the tax rate on current delivery exceeds algebraically the tax rate on contracts for future delivery. It is easily verified that this relation holds for the region $a_i^t > -1$. If, on the other hand, any of the a_i^t terms did not satisfy this condition, it would pay the home country to increase taxes on trade in that good because more imports could be had for fewer exports. This would correspond to the inelastic region of the foreign offer curve in the two-good case, a region in which the home country, as a monopolist, should not operate.

Further, letting $\delta = (P_1^1/P_2^1 - P_1^0/P_2^0)/(P_1^0/P_2^0)$, the percentage rate of appreciation of bread in terms of wine, it can be shown that

$$r_2 - r_1 = \delta(1 - r_1),$$

which is an expression of the Fisherian rule that, ignoring δr_1 as negligible, "two rates of interest in...two diverging standards will, in a perfect adjustment, differ from each other by an amount equal to the rate of divergence between the two standards" (Fisher 1954, p. 39).

The multiperiod, many-good case gives rise to possibilities of substitutability and complementarity at the same point in time and over time. In the simple two-good case, substitution over time is the sole possibility. In both instances the problem of optimum taxes on capital movements, including borrowing and lending, has been treated as a branch of the optimum tariffs. Further, as in tariff theory, the tax depends directly upon the relative monopoly power of the country in world capital markets.

CONCLUSION

When trade is composed not only of the export and import of commodities in the present but also of borrowing and lending over time, it is possible to design a tariff structure and taxes on foreign lending that seek to maximize the home country's well-being at the expense of other countries. This nationalistic trade and lending policy attempts to improve the home country's terms of trade—that is, the relative price of its export goods and the rate of interest at which it borrows or lends. Such a policy may well be shortsighted, however, since other countries may retaliate with restrictions on trade and lending of their own. In any event unfettered foreign trade and lending is, in the absence of decreasing costs and externalities, Pareto optimal from the point of view of the world taken as a whole.

SELECTED READINGS

Connolly, Michael, and Stephen Ross. 1970. "A Fisherian Approach to Trade, Capital Movements, and Tariffs," *American Economic Review* (June).
Dornbusch, Rudiger. 1983. "Real Interest Rates, Home Goods and Optimal External Borrowing." *Journal of Political Economy* (February).
Fisher, Irving. 1954. *The Theory of Interest.* New York: Kelley and Millman.
Graaff, J. de V. 1949. "On Optimal Tariff Structures." *Review of Economic Studies.*
MacDougall, G. D. A. 1960. "The Benefits and Costs of Private Investment from Abroad: A Theoretical Approach." *Economic Record* (March).

INDEX

AUTHOR INDEX

SUBJECT INDEX

ABOUT THE AUTHOR

MICHAEL CONNOLLY is a Professor of Economics at the University of South Carolina. He has held previous teaching positions at Harvard University, the University of Florida, and the Johns Hopkins Bologna Center. He has been Visiting Professor at the Université de Paris–Dauphine, France; the Graduate Institute of International Studies, Geneva, Switzerland; the University of Uppsala, Sweden; the Centre Universitaire des Antilles, Martinique; and the University of Miami.

His articles have appeared in the *American Economic Review*, the *Journal of Political Economy*, the *Quarterly Journal of Economics*, the *Journal of Money, Credit and Banking*, the *Journal of International Money and Finance*, and the *Journal of International Economics*. He coedited *International Trade and Money* (Allen & Unwin, 1973) and the *Economics of the Caribbean Basin* (Praeger, 1985).

Dr. Connolly has a B.A. degree in economics from the University of California at Berkeley and an M.A. and Ph.D. in economics from the University of Chicago.